The Lonely Londoners

Samuel Selvon

with an introduction by Kenneth Ramchand
Professor of West Indian Literature University of the West
Indies

 LONGMAN

Addison Wesley Longman Limited
Edinburgh Gate, Harlow,
Essex CM20 2JE, England
and Associated Companies throughout the world.

Carlong Publishers (Caribbean) Limited
P.O. Box 489, Kingston 10,
33 Second Street, Newport West,
Kingston 13, Jamaica

Lexicon Trinidad Ltd,
Boundary Road, San Juan, Trinidad

Copp Clark Longman, 2775 Matheson Blvd East,
Mississauga, Ontario L4W 4P7

Longman Publishing Group
10 Bank Street, White Plains,
New York 10601-1951, USA

First published by Alan Wingate 1956
First published in Longman Caribbean Writers Series 1985
Sixteenth impression 1998

ISBN 0 582 64264.7

Printed in China
PPLC/16

An Introduction to this Novel

Selvon's *The Lonely Londoners* (1956) is usually grouped with a number of works that help to form a picture of the lives of West Indians and descendants of West Indians in the United Kingdom. Of these, the earliest is Jean Rhys's novel, *Voyage in the Dark* (1934), our first Negritude novel, the story of a girl from the islands adrift in a mean and savage city ("this is London – hundreds thousands of white people rushing along and the dark houses all alike frowning down one after the other all alike and stuck together – the streets like smooth shut-in ravines and the dark houses frowning down – oh I'm not going to like this place I'm not going to like this place ..."). By the mid-1970s, emphases had changed. Linton Kwesi Johnson's *Dread Beat and Blood* (1975) gave soulful expression to the longing and violence of a generation born in England of West Indian parents, with little knowledge or experience of the West Indies, and without an undisputed place in their new homeland.

Between the pre-war period covered by *Voyage in the Dark*, and the emergence of a generation Black and British came the great tide of emigrants "with their cardboard grips and felt hats". Several thousand West Indians had been recruited into the armed forces of Britain, and yet others had been brought in to work in war factories. R.B. Davison traces the effect of this in his *West Indian Migrants* (London: OUP, 1962):

At the end of the war these men returned home to

3

find a disappointing situation. Jobs were hard to find and the standard of living they could expect in their home islands was much lower than that which they had enjoyed in Britain. There were no restrictions on their entry into Britain, for their passports bore witness to the fact that they were 'citizens of the United Kingdom and Colonies'. They began to trickle back to Britain to seek their fortunes and began to write home glowing accounts (backed up by cash remittances) of the varied opportunities available in the booming post-war British economy. Shipping companies, sensing a new avenue for profit, began to offer cheap fares to Britain in vessels returning to Europe and the migration developed rapidly.

In her 'Colonisation in Reverse', the Jamaican Louise Bennett described what was happening in all the islands:

By de hundred, by de t'ousan
From country and from town,
By de ship-load, by the plane-load
Jamaica is Englan boun.

By 1956, when *The Lonely Londoners* was first published, the annual figure for migrants from the West Indies had reached over 25,000. This was the period when extended families would materialise in the thin air of Waterloo Station as a disconcerted Tolroy finds in the following scene from *The Lonely Londoners* (p.29):

A old woman who look like she would dead any minute come out of a carriage, carrying a cardboard box and a paperbag. When she get out the train she stand up there on the platform as if she confuse. Then after she a young girl come, carrying a flourbag filled up with things. Then a young man wearing a widebrim hat and a jacket falling below the knees. Then a little boy and a little girl, then another old woman, tottering so much a guard had was to help she get out of the train.

"Oh Jesus Christ," Tolroy say, "what is this at all?"

"Tolroy," the first woman say, "you don't know your own mother?"

Tolroy hug his mother like a man in a daze, then he say: "But what Tanty Bessy doing here, ma? and Agnes and Lewis and the two children?"

"All of we come, Tolroy," Ma say.

By the mid-1950s the traditional open door policy to Commonwealth citizens began to be questioned, and in November 1961 a Commonwealth Immigrants Bill to restrict this flow was introduced in the House of Commons. The figures for 1960 and the first ten months of 1961 (52,655 and 52,849 respectively) represent a surge of panic arising from anti-immigration rumblings in the United Kingdom. But by this time, too, nobody believed that the streets of London were paved with gold or that the natives were all friendly.

Of the writings that register and describe this movement of West Indian peoples, the conditions they endured after arrival, and the sour-sweet fruit of the several journeys to an expectation, two very different books have become emblematic. George Lamming's collection of essays, *The Pleasures of Exile* (1960), or its title, stands for the attempt to formulate an analysis of the situation as it affected the intellectual or the man of letters; Samuel Selvon's *The Lonely Londoners* focusses on the larger body of immigrants of working-class status, differing further still from *The Pleasures of Exile* in being a work of fiction, an imaginative response to, and rendering of human experience.

Selvon's immigrants are offered the worst jobs; they pay high prices for insecure tenancy in the most undesirable houses, and they indulge in sexual exploits that seldom include anything other than sex. They suffer from rain, snow, wind and fog, and are driven to combine as pirates or parasites on the fringes of a host society which regards them with indifference or hostility. There is also, as Selvon's language can suggest with vividness, the unspoken fear of contamination: "When Moses sit down and pay his fare he take out a *white* handkerchief and blow his nose. The handkerchief turn *black*..." (p. 23) (emphasis added).

The force of race and colour prejudice bearing against the immigrants is shown in incidents, and through conversations, but never without inventiveness or a sense of the human comedy, as in Galahad's apostrophe to the colour black when he wants to understand why he is being treated so:

> And Galahad watch the colour of his hand, and talk to it, saying, "Colour, is you causing all this, you know. Why the hell you can't be blue, or red or green, if you can't be white? You know is you that cause a lot of misery in the world. Is not me, you know, is you! I ain't do anything to infuriate the people and them, is you! Look at you, you so black and innocent, and this time so you causing misery all over the world!"
> So Galahad talking to the colour Black, as if is a person ... (p. 88)

-In two later novels, *The Housing Lark* (1965) and *Moses Ascending* (1975), Selvon returns to the West

Indian experience of London with such fidelity that his work confirms our knowledge of a social evolution within the immigrant population. The exiled body in *The Lonely Londoners* is still very much West Indian; by the time we get to *Moses Ascending* we look through the only partly comprehending eyes, and listen to the deliberately archaic language of an older immigrant as the confused struggle and growing urge towards violence of a new generation are presented. It is a generation that insists on being Black, partly becasue it is not West Indian, and partly because it refuses to be English either by liberal favour or according to any definition of "English" that does not recognise what Defoe, the author of 'The True-Born Englishman' saw even in 1703: such definitions must be continually revised as new and active components make themselves felt.

We could not be sure of the reliability of the kind of information we have been extracting from Selvon's novel if we did not already possess knowledge about West Indian immigration to London in the form of testimonies by migrants, or as a result of research by social scientists and historians. So to praise a novel for its fidelity to social or historical facts is to praise it, as some critics do, for being secondary. Novels characteristically distort and re-shape facts in order to express feelings that are part of the meaning of the facts, feelings that may well be about to lead to a new set of facts.

The Lonely Londoners is a work of imagination. Our understanding of its relevance to the social world from which it draws its material is enhanced by our first responding to it as fiction, something that has been made up, in this case, out of fairly recognisable material. The first paragraph consists of one sentence, and from this ominous opening utterance through whose first half, thick with fog and delaying phrases that fixed and weary traveller Moses Aloetta emerges to board the shuttle once again to the immigrant station, the tone and texture of Selvon's prose begin to signal the approach of an alien planet. A sun without heat hangs in the sky "like a force-ripe orange"; the drifting and lost Galahad has to touch himself all over for the consolation of a familiar reality; and a hand from the empty air falls on his shoulder to immobilize him. One of the inhabitants of the city takes Cap to the back of the station where "All Cap seeing is railway line and big junk of iron all about the yard, and some thick, heavy cable lying around. It have some snow on the ground, and the old fog at home as usual. It look like hell ..." (p. 52). Seeking a footing in this strange inhospitable ground also are even stranger creatures, including "a old woman who look like she would dead any minute," and on a cold winter evening, shambling out of sleep and the last carriage a "miracle of metabolism," the irrepressible phenomenon Henry Oliver, clad in "a old grey tropical suit and a pair of watchekong and no overcoat or muffler or gloves or anything for the cold ..." (p. 32).

Selvon's immigrants inhabit a nightmare world. Having met their Waterloo, "a place of arrival and departure ... a place where you see people crying goodbye and kissing welcome," the immigrants next call upon the employment exchange where, as Moses casually informs the newcomer Galahad, a Jamaican had gone berserk, tearing up files and papers, snatching at a clerk, and swearing and bawling. The narrating voice sadly tells: "It ain't have no place in the world that exactly like a place where a lot of men get together to look for work and draw money from the

Welfare State while they ain't working. Is a kind of place where hate and disgust and avarice and malice and sympathy and sorrow and pity all mix up. Is a place where everyone is your enemy and your friend" (p. 45).

It is worth noticing that many of the details that go to make up the deathly universe of *The Lonely Londoners* are present in V.S. Naipaul's *The Mimic Men*, too. In describing the reducing effects of the city, for example, Ralph Singh, the first-person narrator, speaks of people being "trapped into fixed postures," of "the personality divided bewilderingly into compartments," and of "the panic of ceasing to feel myself as a whole person." Selvon's third-person narrating voice sees London as a place "divide up in little worlds, and you stay in the world you belong to and you don't know about what happening in the other ones except what you read in the papers." (p. 74) If none of Selvon's characters experiences the psychic crash that Ralph Singh suffers, the book nevertheless abounds with examples of hysteria, eccentricity and irresponsible non-moral behaviour. The insecure Lewis develops a fixation that his wife entertains lovers while he is on night-shift; Harris puts on proper English three-piece suit, bowler hat, umbrella and briefcase, and lives in constant fear of being embarrassed by his less conforming countrymen; a haggard and haunted Bart combs the city hoping to find his lost love Beatrice; the smiling Cap's innocent face masks a ruthless determination to survive and exploit in a world that has neither meaning nor structure; and "Moses sigh a long sigh like a man who live life and see nothing at all in it and who frighten as the years go by wondering what it is all about" (p. 110).

It is useful to notice that the positives in Naipaul's

9

sad story have to be extracted from the book by means of a careful discrimination between Ralph Singh's character (the kind of victim Naipaul shows him to be) and his function (the times when Naipaul allows him to say things that strike us as authoritative although they don't proceed from or in any way modify his essential character). The positives in Selvon's book, in contrast, emerge fairly directly through the author's use of an experienced, compassionate, and reflective third-person narrator.

But it has become usual to speak of the narrator's stance in *The Lonely Londoners* as being similar to that of a calypsonian, a harmless enough fancy had it not been accompanied by a willingness to concede that this book is loose or episodic. The examination questions reflecting this approach covertly invite students to argue that the work relates to the oral tradition and that in performance it is given shape and coherence by the teller who is present to the audience throughout. Beware, the implied argument seems to run, beware of using Eurocentric critical tools to assess our literature.

To discuss the narrator, and by inevitable extension, the narrating technique of *The Lonely Londoners* is to engage in an enterprise that leads us to appreciate the book as writing, specifically, a novel. From looking at the narrator we are drawn to recognise in Selvon's literary artefact a tightness of structure (the way the parts are put inevitably together); subtlety in the development and revelation of theme; linguistic cunning; and an appropriateness in the presentation and deployment of characters. The work is an admirable illustration of how writing can feed on oral literature and on the stuff that oral literature itself also draws upon without losing its identity as writing.[1]

The narrating voice in *The Lonely Londoners* reports

vividly on who does what when: "One grim winter evening, when it had a kind of unrealness about London, with a fog sleeping restlessly over the city and the lights showing in the blur as if is not London at all but some strange place on another planet, Moses Aloetta hop on a number 46 bus at the corner of Chepstow Road and Westbourne Grove to go to Waterloo to meet a fellar who was coming from Trinidad on the boat-train" (p. 23). After describing the meeting between the established immigrant and the cocky new arrival, Henry Oliver, the narrating voice rises to mock-heroic: "Thus it was that Henry Oliver Esquire, alias Sir Galahad, descend on London to swell the population by one, and eight and a half months later it had a Galahad junior in Ladbroke Grove ..." (p. 35). In the sequence describing London (pp. 73-76) the narrating voice becomes that of someone who has seen and suffered much. He knows men ("It have a kind of fellar ..." p. 38) and he knows something of the world (It ain't have no place in the world that ..." p. 45).

Gradually, the voice becomes a person. Although he is not described physically, he becomes a solid presence taking the reader through a shattering world. A moving account (p. 66) of Bart's desolation and his desperate, enthralled search just for the sight of Beatrice ends with acceptance and a quiet awe: "It have men like that in the world, too." When summer comes, he can exult like one of the boys, "for then the sun shine for true and the sky blue and a warm wind blowing it look like when is winter a kind of grey nasty colour does come to the sky and it stay there and you forget what it like to see blue skies like back home where blue sky so common people don't even look up in the air and you feeling miserable and cold but when summer come is fire in the town big times fete like stupidness and you have to keep the blood cool ..." (p. 102). Like the boys, he exults without forgetting winter, and his present enjoyment is tinged with nostalgia for the year-long summer of the islands; unlike the boys he is conscious of and articulate about this complex of feelings.

The narrating person then, has not lost the capacity for joy nor humane feeling. If the world sometimes puzzles him, there is a wise acceptance of hidden springs ("Things does have a way of fixing themselves") and outer limits ("in the end everybody dead" p. 67). Unlike Ralph Singh, who withdraws from the cycle of events ("from our respective countries, from the city where we find ourselves, from our families" ... and "from unnecessary responsibility and attachment"), the engaged and thinking narrator of *The Lonely Londoners* returns again and again to a belief in the possibility of meaning. When Cap of all persons decides to take a wife, there is a philosophical response which incidentally throws light also on Selvon's plotting, or ordering of the sequence of the book:

> who can tell what was the vap that hit Cap and make him get married? A man like he, who ain't have nothing, no clothes, no work, no house to live in, no place to go? Yet is so things does happen in life. You work things out in your own mind to a kind of pattern, in a sort of sequence, and one day bam! something happen to throw everything out of gear, what you expect to happen never happen, what you don't expect to happen always happen, and you have to start thinking all over again. (p. 56)

We come to depend upon the narrating person as chronicler, repository of the experiences of the group, and as the ideal and attuned sensibility.

This is in part, and at root, a linguistic achievement. For as the quotations above show, the narrating voice varies in vocabulary and in grammar and syntax to suit differing situations. To make up this flexible language, Selvon draws expertly upon the whole linguistic spectrum available to the literate West Indian, ranging from English Standard English to West Indian Standard English to differing degrees of dialect, inventing new combinations and adding his own emphases. The language of *The Lonely Londoners* is not the language of one stratum in the society, not the language of the people meaning 'the folk' or the peasantry, but a careful fabrication, a modified dialect which contains and expresses the sensibility of a whole society.

But Selvon has more complications for the narrating person. *The Lonely Londoners* contains a character who can only be described as the central character, and Selvon structures the book in such a way as to make it the story of what happens to Moses with the passing of time. The episodes/ballads seem to issue forth with oral spontaneity, but from the first meeting at Waterloo between the new conquering migrant Henry Galahad Oliver and his reluctant, fascinated mentor, the Moses who has already served ten years in the metropolis, an unobtrusive but tight narrative design declares itself. There is a forward action in the novel covering the first two or three years of Galahad's life in the city, his relationship with Moses and his relationship with "the boys" during this time. But also, in flashback (pp. 47-66, 93-98 for example) and by direct comparison or allusion between the now and the early days, we get an account of Moses' arrival and settlement in London.

As the reliable and sympathetic narrating voice tries

to explain, the Moses who waits in the station for Galahad has already drifted into stasis: "It was here that Moses did land when he came to London, and he have no doubt that when the time come, if it ever come, it would be here he would say goodbye to the big city. Perhaps he was thinking is time to go back to the tropics, that's why he feeling sort of lonely and miserable" (p. 26). Moses tries to persuade Galahad "to hustle a passage back home to Trinidad today," and throughout the book the veteran produces "a knowing smile," "a tired smile," "a weary look," or the advice to "Take it easy" as the excited newcomer reports on his first experience of things to which the experienced immigrant has become inured and unresponsive. Moses' knowledge of life in London (he has seen and/ or suffered almost everything in his time) allows him to indulge in a superior irony over Galahad.

But a larger irony works in the opposite direction. Galahad is one in whom the zest for life and the capacity for romance are unquenchable. The fulfilling romance of the city is epitomized for Galahad in the phrase "Charing Cross" (p. 84), or in this heady response to Piccadilly Circus:

Always, from the first time he went there to see Eros and the lights, that circus have a magnet for him, that circus represent life, that circus is the beginning and ending of the world. Every time he go there, he have the same feeling like when he see it the first night, drink coca-cola, any time is guinness time, bovril and the fireworks, a million flashing lights, gay laughter, the wide doors of theatres, the huge posters, everready batteries, rich people going into tall hotels, people going to the theatre, people sitting and standing and walking and talking and laughing and buses and cars and Galahad Esquire, in all this, standing there in the big city, in London. Oh Lord. (p. 90)

Introducing Galahad to London life, Moses is obliged to relive past experiences. Heavy with *déjà vu*, he resorts to irony and amused tolerance. But the reader sees that even if Galahad is to suffer disillusion, Moses has lost something vital. With metropolitan pressure, the Galahad in himself has faded. So the author's irony emerges to point to a Moses whose consciousness is to become further troubled, and to assert the Galahad value:

"What do you think, Moses?" he ask Moses.
    "Ah, in you I see myself when I was new in London. All them places is like nothing to me now. Is like when you go back home and you hear fellars talk about Times Square and Fifth Avenue, and Charing Cross and gay Paree. You say to yourself, 'Lord, them places must be sharp.' Then you get a chance and you see them for yourself, and is like nothing."
    "You remember that picture *Waterloo Bridge*, with Robert Taylor? I went down by the bridge the other night, and stand up and watch the river."
    "Take it easy," Moses say wearily.
    But Galahad feel like a king living in London.
(p. 85)

Galahad's relentless faith in life forces Moses to realize, beyond the possibility of easy irony, the extent of the losses that he bears. From this point Moses (altered ego) is more patient with Galahad, and becomes more anxious to find words to explain his growing introspections. And in the free-flowing prose-poem about summer (pp. 101-110), there is a double narrative, Selvon superimposing the account of Moses's initiation of Galahad into the joys of summer upon an evocation of Moses's own time of delight ("coasting about the water it ain't have no man with a sharper eye than he not even Cap could ask him for anything"). The passage ends with Moses's fear of the emptiness time leaves, and through which it passes, but co-existing with this attitude is a celebratory tone associated with the positive assertion of life represented by Galahad:

> all these things happen in the blazing summer
> under the trees in the park on the grass with the
> daffodils and tulips in full bloom and a sky of blue
> oh it does really be beautiful then to hear the birds
> whistling and see the green leaves come back on the
> trees and in the night the world turn upside down
> and everybody hustling that is life that is London oh
> lord Galahad say when the sweetness of summer get
> in him he say he would never leave the old Brit'n as
> long as he live and Moses sigh a long sigh like a man
> who live life and see nothing at all in it and who
> frighten as the years go by wondering what it is all
> about. (p. 109)

The excitement that has faded for Moses was not an illusion. Moses is not Ralph Singh. If Naipaul in *The Mimic Men* describes a process of shrinkage, Selvon through Moses essays towards painful growth.

Moses's process (for he is the central character in what is after all a novel), his development as a character, comes to its real climax in the last two pages of the novel. But before looking at this we have to study the relationship between Moses's point of view and that of the narrating person.

In the early pages, when the narrating voice is establishing Moses as a character, the difference between the two is obvious; and it has been shown above how the author's irony works to modify Moses's solemn perspective. But in a large number of scenes, the narrative point of view is shared between Moses who is present (we see and hear what he does), and the narrator who comments or elaborates on the scene out of a larger knowledge, and more developed consciousness. As the novel draws to a close, however, there is a significant identification between narrator and the growing central character.

A movement running from page 121 through to the end of the novel may be used to demonstrate. In five paragraphs, beginning with "The changing of the seasons ..." the narrating voice celebrates the Galahad capacity for romance and delight; maturely recognises the constructions men must live with, refusing to reject the romance of the city or of life; and then focuses on how "the boys" are making out in the city. The snatches of conversation mark a cross over from the narrator's perspective to Moses's point of view (Sometimes during the week, when he come home and he can't sleep, is as if he hearing the voices in the room ..."). The "boys" come to his room "like if they going to church", telling their anecdotes "like if is confession". Their woes haunt Moses whose imagination and compassion now are no different from those of the charged narrator:

> Sometimes during the week, when he come home and he can't sleep, is as if he hearing the voices in the room, all the moaning and groaning and sighing and crying, and he open his eyes expecting to see the boys sitting around.

Sometimes, listening to them, he look in each face,
and he feel a great compassion for every one of
them, as if he live each of their lives, one by one,
and all the strain and stress come to rest on his own
shoulders (p. 138).

The identification between Moses and the narrator
is described in other terms by Gordon Rohlehr: "Moses
by the end of the book has a high priest's role ... a
repository for group consciousness, a sort of archetypal
old man, a Tiresias figure." (*Critics on Caribbean
Literature*, ed. Baugh, p. 161). And although Rohlehr
notices that Moses contemplates at the end "the
aimlessness of things", he prefers to point to a
"technique of moving from a fragmentary form, where
several voices share the stage, to a point where all the
voices are blended either in chorus as in Mais's *Brother
Man* or into the single representative voice of an
archetypal figure ...".

Attractive as this might be as an abstraction, it does
not seem to me to catch Selvon's emphasis and tone or
describe what happens to Moses. For more important
than being blended in chorus is the process which the
whole book may be said to be about – Moses's
individuation, and his emergence as a thinking
creature:

The old Moses, standing on the banks of the
Thames. Sometimes he think he see some sort of
profound realisation in his life, as if all that happen
to him was experience that make him a better man,
as if now he could draw apart from any hustling and
just sit down and watch other people fight to live.
Under the kiff-kiff laughter, behind the ballad and
the episode, the what-happening, the summer-is-
hearts, he could see a great aimlessness, a great
restless, swaying movement that leaving you

standing in the same spot. As if a forlorn shadow of doom fall on all the spades in the country. As if he could see the black faces bobbing up and down in the millions of white, strained faces, everybody hustling along the Strand, the spades jostling in the crowd, bewildered, hopeless. As if, on the surface, things don't look so bad, but when you go down a little, you bounce up a kind of misery and pathos and a frightening – what? He don't know the right word, but he have the right feeling in his heart. As if the boys laughing, but they only laughing because they fraid to cry, they only laughing because to think so much about everything would be a big calamity – like how he here now, the thoughts so heavy like he unable to move his body. (p. 141)

Selvon's modified dialect rises to an occasion that *The Lonely Londoners* wishes to celebrate. The energy and optimism of the group are presented as great positives, and the figure of Galahad is a poignant reminder of something that is going out of the world. For Selvon, however, it is only through the development of consciousness that the group, tribe, clan, community or whatever, can preserve its essential qualities while living as twentieth-century people. A defensive regression into the unthinking group is no better than the withdrawal into the tomb of Ralph Singh. For Moses, and presumably for Selvon, the birth of consciousness is the beginning of our participation in the perennial effort to sing simultaneously our songs of innocence and experience:

Still, it had a greatness and a vastness in the way he was feeling tonight, like it was something solid after feeling everything else give way, and though he ain't getting no happiness out of the cogitations he still pondering, for is the first time he ever find himself thinking like that. (p. 142)

At this elated moment, the narrator, Moses, and Sam Selvon the author seem to fuse into one in the urge towards articulation and writing:

> Daniel was telling him how over in France all kinds of fellars writing books what turning out to be best-sellers. Taxi-driver, porter, road-sweeper – it didn't matter. One day you sweating in the factory and the next day all the newspapers have your name and photo, saying how you are a new literary giant.
>
> He watch a tugboat on the Thames, wondering if he could ever write a book like that, what everybody would buy.[2]

Kenneth Ramchand
Professor of West Indian
Literature, University of the West Indies

[1]   The present introduction is a reworking of an earlier piece 'The Lonely Londoners as a Literary Work' in *World Literature Written in English*, Autumn 1982, pp. 56-64. The argument about writing and orality is conducted at greater length in 'The Fate of Writing in the West Indies', *Caribbean Review*, Vol. XI, No 4, 1982 pp. 16-17 and 40-41.

[2]   In a sense, *The Lonely Londoners* is the book Moses would have written.

In two later books, *Moses Ascending* (1975) and *Moses Migrating* (1983), Selvon uses a main character called Moses. This has given rise to some loose talk about a Moses trilogy which is not only wrong but misleading. There is a similarity between the Moses of *Moses Ascending* and the Moses of *Moses Migrating*, and there is a continuity between the two books which can justify us in seeing the one as a sequel to the other, and regarding the two Moses characters as one character at different stages. But the Moses at the end of *The Lonely Londoners* is akin to Tiger of *A Brighter Sun* and Foster of *An Island is a world*, characters who are seeking answers to profound questions with an intensity that suggests a closeness to the author, and a challenge to the author which the Moses of ... *Ascending* and ... *Migrating* hardly poses. While the latter books are amusing, they suggest a disengagement by the author from his protagonist which at times, especially at the climax of *Moses Migrating*, feels like cynicism or evasion.

ONE GRIM winter evening, when it had a kind of unrealness about London, with a fog sleeping restlessly over the city and the lights showing in the blur as if is not London at all but some strange place on another planet, Moses Aloetta hop on a number 46 bus at the corner of Chepstow Road and Westbourne Grove to go to Waterloo to meet a fellar who was coming from Trinidad on the boat-train.

When Moses sit down and pay his fare he take out a white handkerchief and blow his nose. The handkerchief turn black and Moses watch it and curse the fog. He wasn't in a good mood and the fog wasn't doing anything to help the situation. He had was to get up from a nice warm bed and dress and come out in this nasty weather to go and meet a fellar that he didn't even know. That was the hurtful part of it—is not as if this fellar is his brother or cousin or even friend; he don't know the man from Adam. But he get a letter from a friend in Trinidad who say that this fellar coming by the ss *Hildebrand*, and if he could please meet him at the station in London, and help him until he get settled. The fellar name Henry Oliver, but the friend tell Moses not to worry that he describe Moses to Henry, and all he have to do is to be in the station when the boat-train pull in and this fellar Henry would find him. So for old time sake Moses find himself on the bus going to Waterloo, vex with himself that his heart so soft that he always doing something for somebody and nobody ever doing anything for him.

Because it look to Moses that he hardly have time to settle in the old Brit'n before all sorts of fellars start coming straight to his room in the Water when they land up in London from the

West Indies, saying that so and so tell them that Moses is a good fellar to contact, that he would help them get place to stay and work to do.

'Jesus Christ,' Moses tell Harris, a friend he have, 'I never see thing so. I don't know these people at all, yet they coming to me as if I is some liaison officer, and I catching my arse as it is, how I could help them out?'

And this sort of thing was happening at a time when the English people starting to make rab about how too much West Indians coming to the country: this was a time, when any corner you turn, is ten to one you bound to bounce up a spade. In fact, the boys all over London, it ain't have a place where you wouldn't find them, and big discussion going on in Parliament about the situation, though the old Brit'n too diplomatic to clamp down on the boys or to do anything drastic like stop them from coming to the Mother Country. But big headlines in the papers every day, and whatever the newspaper and the radio say in this country, that is the people Bible. Like one time when newspapers say that the West Indians think that the streets of London paved with gold a Jamaican fellar went to the income tax office to find out something and first thing the clerk tell him is, 'You people think the streets of London are paved with gold?' Newspaper and radio rule this country.

Now the position have Moses uneasy, because to tell truth most of the fellars who coming now are real hustlers, desperate; it not like long time when forty or fifty straggling in, they invading the country by the hundreds. And when them fellars who here a long time see people running from the West Indies, is only logic for them to say it would be damn foolishness to go back. So what Moses could do when these fellars land up hopeless on the doorstep with one set of luggage, no place to sleep, no place to go?

One day a set of fellars come.

'Who tell you my name and address?' Moses ask them.

'Oh, we get it from a fellar name Jackson who was up here last year.'

'Jackson is a bitch,' Moses say, 'he know that I seeing hell myself.'

'We have money,' the fellars say, 'we only want you to help we to get a place to stay and tell we how to get a work.'

'That harder than money,' Moses grunt. 'I don't know why the hell you come to me.' But all the same he went out with them, because he used to remember how desperate he was when he was in London for the first time and didn't know anybody or anything.

Moses send the boys to different addresses. 'Too much spades in the Water now,' he tell them. 'Try down by Clapham. You don't know how to get there? They will tell you in the tube station. Also, three of you could go to King's Cross station and ask for a fellar name Samson who working in the luggage department. He will help you out.'

And so like a welfare officer Moses scattering the boys around London, for he don't want no concentrated area in the Water— as it is, things bad enough already. And one or two that he take a fancy to, he take them around by houses he know it would be all right to go to, for at this stage Moses know which part they will slam door in your face and which part they will take in spades.

And is the same soft heart that have him now on the bus going to Waterloo to meet a fellar name Henry Oliver. He don't know how he always getting in position like this, helping people out. He sigh; the damn bus crawling in the fog, and the evening so melancholy that he wish he was back in bed.

When he get to Waterloo he hop off and went in the station, and right away in that big station he had a feeling of homesickness that he never felt in the nine-ten years he in this country. For the old Waterloo is a place of arrival and departure, is a place where you see people crying goodbye and kissing welcome, and he hardly have time to sit down on a bench before this

feeling of nostalgia hit him and he was surprise. It have some
fellars who in Brit'n long, and yet they can't get away from the
habit of going Waterloo whenever a boat-train coming in with
passengers from the West Indies. They like to see the familiar
faces, they like to watch their countrymen coming off the train,
and sometimes they might spot somebody they know: 'Aye
Watson! What the hell you doing in Brit'n boy? Why you didn't
write me you was coming?' And they would start big oldtalk
with the travellers, finding out what happening in Trinidad, in
Grenada, in Barbados, in Jamaica and Antigua, what is the
latest calypso number, if anybody dead, and so on, and even
asking strangers question they can't answer, like if they know
Tanty Simmons who living Labasse in Port of Spain, or a fellar
name Harrison working in the Red House.

But Moses, he never in this sort of slackness: the thought
never occur to him to go to Waterloo just to see who coming up
from the West Indies. Still, the station is that sort of place
where you have a soft feeling. It was here that Moses did land
when he come to London, and he have no doubt that when the
time come, if it ever come, it would be here he would say goodbye to the big city. Perhaps he was thinking is time to go back
to the tropics, that's why he feeling sort of lonely and miserable.

Moses was sitting there on a bench, smoking a Woods, when
a Jamaican friend name Tolroy come up.

'The boat-train come yet?' Tolroy ask, though he know it
ain't come yet.

'No,' Moses say, though he know that Tolroy know.

'Boy, I expect my mother to come,' Tolroy say, in a nervous
way, as if he frighten at the idea.

'You send for she?' Moses say.

'Yes,' Tolroy say.

'Ah, I wish I was like allyou Jamaican,' Moses say, 'Allyou
could live on two-three pound a week, and save up money in a
suitcase under the bed, then when you have enough you sending
for the family. I can't save a cent out of my pay.'

'What I do is my business,' Tolroy say, taking offence.

'Yes, I ain't say is a bad thing, I trying to do the same thing ever since I come to this country. I was just thinking bout when you yourself did first come, how I help you to get a job in the factory, and how you have so much money save and I ain't have cent. So it go, boy. You still living Harrow Road?'

'Yes. But now the old lady coming I will have to look for a bigger place. You know about any?'

'Not my way. But Big City was telling me yesterday it have a house down by the Grove what have some vacant rooms—why you don't see him and find out?'

'I will see him tomorrow. You have a cigarette?'

'I just smoking the last.'

Tolroy sit down on the bench with Moses, and the two of them watching Waterloo station, all the things that happening, all the people that coming and going.

'Where the guitar?' Moses ask.

'I didn't bring it, man,' Tolroy say.

When Tolroy did left Jamaica he bring a guitar with him to Brit'n, and he always have this guitar with him, playing it in the road and in the tube, and when he standing up in the queues.

'We better get platform ticket,' Moses say, and they was just in time, for the boat-train pull in and people start to come off the train. Moses stand up out of the way with his hands in his pocket, not interested in the passengers, only waiting for this fellar Henry to come so he could get back home out of the cold and the fog.

It had a Jamaican fellar who living in Brixton, that come to the station to see what tenants he could pick up for the houses that he have in Brixton. This test when he did first come open up a club, and by and by he save up money and buy a house. The next thing you know, he buy out a whole street of houses in Brixton, and let out rooms to the boys, hitting them anything like three or four guineas for a double. When it come to making

money, it ain't have anything like 'ease me up' or 'both of we
is countrymen together' in the old London. Sometimes he put
bed and chair in two or three big room and tell the fellars they
could live in there together, but each would have to pay a
pound. So you could imagine—five-six fellars in one room and
the test coining money for so. And whenever a boat-train come
in, he hustling down to Waterloo to pick up them fellars who
new to London and ain't have place to stay, telling them how
Brixton is a nice area, that it have plenty Jamaicans down there
already, and they would feel at home in the district, because the
Mayor on the boys' side and it ain't have plenty prejudice there.

While Moses smiling to see the test hustling tenants, a newspaper fellar come up to him and say, 'Excuse me sir, have you
just arrived from Jamaica?'

And Moses don't know why but he tell the fellar yes.

'Would you like to tell me what conditions there are like?'
The fellar take out notebook and pencil and look at Moses.

Now Moses don't know a damn thing about Jamaica—Moses
come from Trinidad, which is a thousand miles from Jamaica,
but the English people believe that everybody who come from the
West Indies come from Jamaica.

'The situation is desperate,' Moses say, thinking fast, 'you
know the big hurricane it had two weeks ago?'

'Yes?' the reporter say, for in truth it did have a hurricane in
Jamaica.

'Well I was in that hurricane,' Moses say. 'Plenty people get
kill. I was sitting down in my house and suddenly when I look
up I see the sky. What you think happen?'

'What?'

'The hurricane blow the roof off.'

'But tell me, sir, why are so many Jamaicans immigrating to
England?'

'Ah,' Moses say, 'that is a question to limit, that is what everybody trying to find out. They can't get work,' Moses say,
warming up. 'And furthermore, let me give you my view of

28

the situation in this country. We can't get no place to live, and we only getting the worse jobs it have—'

But by this time the infant feel that he get catch with Moses, and he say, 'Thank you,' and hurry off.

Moses was sorry, it was the first time he ever really get a good chance to say his mind, and he had a lot of things to say. Though one time they wanted to take out his photo. It happen while he was working in a railway yard, and all the people in the place say they go strike unless the boss fire Moses. It was a big ballad in all the papers, they put it under a big headline, saying how the colour bar was causing trouble again, and a fellar come with a camera and wanted to take Moses photo, but Moses say no. A few days after that the boss call Moses and tell him that he sorry, but as they cutting down the staff and he was new, he would have to go.

Meanwhile Tolroy gone down by the bottom of the train, stumbling over suitcase and baggage as he trying to see everybody what coming off the train at the same time.

A old woman who look like she would dead any minute come out of a carriage, carrying a cardboard box and a paperbag. When she get out the train she stand up there on the platform as if she confuse. Then after she a young girl come, carrying a flourbag filled up with things. Then a young man wearing a widebrim hat and a jacket falling below the knees. Then a little boy and a little girl, then another old woman, tottering so much a guard had was to help she get out of the train.

'Oh Jesus Christ,' Tolroy say, 'what is this at all?'

'Tolroy,' the first woman say, 'you don't know your own mother?'

Tolroy hug his mother like a man in a daze, then he say: 'But what Tanty Bessy doing here, ma? and Agnes and Lewis and the two children?'

'All of we come, Tolroy,' Ma say. 'This is how it happen: when you write home to say you getting five pounds a week Lewis say, "Oh God, I going England tomorrow." Well Agnes say that she not staying at home alone with the children, so all of we come.'

'And what about Tanty?'

'Well you know how old your Tanty getting, Tolroy, is a shame to leave she alone to dead in Kingston with nobody to look after she.'

'Oh God ma, why you bring all these people with you?' Tolroy start to shiver with a kind of fright.

'Ah, you see what I tell you?' Tanty say to the mother, 'you see how ungrateful he is? I would go back to Jamaica right now,' and she make as if she going back inside the train.

'Tolroy,' Ma say, 'you remember when you was a little boy how you used to live at Tanty and she used to mind you and send you to school and give you tea and bake in the evening? You remember them days? When Tanty give you shoes to wear and pants to put on your backside? How you expect me to leave Tanty behind when all the family going England?'

'But ma you don't know what you put yourself in,' Tolroy start to argue right there on the platform, and people watching them. A porter pushing a trolley say: 'Come on there, out of the way,' and he nearly bounce up Tanty, who was looking all about in the station with she eyes open wide.

'Look at trouble here!' Tanty say. 'Mister, you best hads mind what you doing, yes. If you touch me with that thing I call a policeman for you.'

Tolroy pull all the family out of the way, and they stand up there arguing, for Tolroy ain't catch himself yet, he can't realise that all these people on his hands, in London, in the grim winter, and no place to go to stay.

The reporter fellar see this small crowd and he figure that it look like a family and he might get a good story from them why so much Jamaican coming to London, so he went up to Tanty and say: 'Excuse me, lady, I am from the *Echo*. Is this your first trip to England?'

'Don't tell that man nothing,' Tolroy growl.

'Why you so prejudice?' Tanty say. 'The gentleman ask me a good question, why I shouldn't answer?' And she turn to the reporter and say, 'Yes mister, is my first trip.'

'Have you any relatives here? Are you going to live in London?'

'Well my nephew Tolroy here in this country a long time, and so he send for the rest of the family to come and live with him. Not so Tolroy?'

But Tolroy gone to help Lewis and Agnes find their luggage.

'Tolroy is a good boy,' Tanty say, 'I mind him since he was small—'

'Yes,' the reporter say, 'but can you tell me why so many people are leaving Jamaica and coming to England?'

'Is the same thing I say.' Tanty say excited, 'I tell all of them who coming, "Why all you leaving the country to go to England? Over there it so cold that only white people does live there." But they say that it have more work in England, and better pay. And to tell you the truth, when I hear that Tolroy getting five pound a week, I had to agree.'

'Tell me madam, what will you do in London?'

'Who me?' Tanty look around as if the reporter talking to somebody else. 'Why. I come to look after the family. All of them was coming, so I had to come too, to look after them. Who will cook and wash the clothes and clean the house?'

This time so, Ma pulling Tanty hand to make she stop talking, but Tanty only shaking off the hand.

'What happening to you?' Tanty tell Ma. 'You can't see this gentleman from the newspapers come to meet we by the station? We have to show that we have good manners, you know.'

'May I take your picture?' the reporter ask.

'He want to take photo,' Tanty nudge Ma. 'Where all the children? Tolroy, Agnes, Lewis,' she calling out as if she calling out in a backyard in Jamaica, 'all you come and take photo, children. The mister want a snapshot.'

'One of you alone will be quite sufficient,' the reporter say.

'What!' Tanty say, 'you can't take me alone. You have to take the whole family.' And she went to round up the rest.

Now Tolroy don't want to have no part in this business but Tanty insisting so much that not so make a bigger scene—people standing up and watching them—he went and stand by Ma with a sulky face.

'Wait a minute,' Tanty tell the reporter when he was ready, and she begin to open up the cardboard box right there on the platform, and she take out a straw hat with a wide brim and put it on she head. 'I ready now,' she say, posing with the family.

'I hope you don't find our weather too cold for you,' the reporter say maliciously when he was going.

The next day when the *Echo* appear it had a picture, and under the picture write: Now, Jamaican Families Come to Britain.

While all this confusion happening Moses was killing himself with laugh, but as all the people begin to go away and he can't see this Henry Oliver—at least nobody ain't broach him—he was just making up his mind to go home when he spot a test straggling up from the bottom of the train as if he did fall asleep and not know the train reach Waterloo.

And in truth is that what happen to Henry, and though he tell some fellars in the carriage to wake him up when they reach London, in the hustlement of getting off the train nobody remember Henry and a guard had was to wake him up.

Moses watch Henry coming up the platform, and he have a feeling that this couldn't be the fellar that he come to meet, for the test have on a old grey tropical suit and a pair of watche-kong and no overcoat or muffler or gloves or anything for the cold, so Moses sure is some test who living in London a long, long time and accustom to the beast winter. Even so, he really had to feel the fellar, for as the evening advancing it getting colder and colder and Moses stamping he foot as he stand up there.

The fellar, as soon as he see Moses, walk straight up to him and say, 'Ah, I bet you is Moses!'

Moses say, 'Yes.'

'Ah,' Henry say, looking about the desolate station as if he in an exhibition hall on a pleasant summer evening. 'Frank did say you would come to meet me in Waterloo. My name Henry Oliver.'

'You not feeling cold, old man?' Moses say, eyeing the specimen with amazement, for he himself have on long wool underwear and a heavy fireman coat that he pick up in Portobello Road.

'No,' Henry say, looking surprise. 'This is the way the weather does be in the winter? It not so bad, man. In fact I feeling a little warm.'

'Jesus Christ,' Moses say. 'What happen to you, you sick or something?'

'Who, me? Sick? Ha-ha, you making joke!'

Moses watch the specimen again suspiciously.

'You must be have on bags of wool under that suit,' he say. 'You can't fool a old test like me.'

'What you making so much fuss about?' Henry say, opening his shirt to show bare skin underneath. 'This is a nice climate, boy. You feeling cold?'

'Take it easy,' Moses say, deciding to wait and see how things would develop with this strange character. 'Get your luggage and we will go. Tonight you could stay by me, but tomorrow I might shift from my room and go upstairs, and I will see if I could fix up with the landlord for you to take my room.'

'Whenever you ready,' Henry say.

'Where your luggage?'

'What luggage? I ain't have any. I figure is no sense to load up myself with a set of things. When I start a work I will buy some things.'

Now Moses is a veteran, who living in this country for a long time, and he meet all sorts of people and do all sorts of things, but he never thought the day would come when a fellar would land up from the sunny tropics on a powerful winter evening wearing a tropical suit and saying that he ain't have no luggage.

'You mean you come from Trinidad with nothing?'

'Well the old toothbrush always in the pocket,' Henry pat the jacket pocket, 'and I have on a pair of pyjamas. Don't worry, I will get fix up as soon as I start to work.'

'You does smoke?'

'Yes. You have any on you now? I finish my last packet on the train.'

'You mean to say you come off the ship with no cigarettes? You don't know they does allow you to land with two hundred, and that it have fellars who manage to come with five-six hundred? You don't know how cigarettes expensive like hell in this country? Nobody tell you anything at all about London? Frank ain't give you some tips before you leave Trinidad?'

'Oh, he tell me a lot of things, but you know how them fellars always like to exaggerate, and I only listen to him halfway.'

'You does drink?'

'Yes.'

'You mean to say you come off the ship with no rum? You don't know they does allow you to land with two bottles, and some of the boys does manage to come ashore with four or five, getting other people who ain't have none to bring it for them? You know how much a bottle of rum does cost in London?'

'How much?'

'Thirty seven and six.'

'How much that is in Trinidad money?'

'Only about ten dollars.'

Henry whistle phew.

'You bring any money?' Moses went on, for by this time he not even sure it ain't a dream he dreaming and he would wake up in bed and laugh at it.

'I have three pounds,' Henry say defensively. 'But ease me up with the questions old man, I tired after that long journey.'

'Is five pounds you could land with, you know.'

'Yes, but I get in a wapee game on board with some of the fellars and lose two. Boy it had a wapee test on board—'

'All right Sir Galahad,' Moses say. 'Take it easy. London will do for you before long. Come, we will catch the tube as you ain't have any luggage.'

Thus it was that Henry Oliver Esquire, alias Sir Galahad, descend on London to swell the population by one, and eight and a half months later it had a Galahad junior in Ladbroke Grove and all them English people stopping in the road and admiring the baby curly hair when the mother pushing it in the pram as she go shopping for rations.

*   *   *

'The only thing,' Galahad say when they was in the tube going to the Water, 'is that I find when I talk smoke coming out my mouth.'

'Is so it is in this country,' Moses say. 'Sometimes the words freeze and you have to melt it to hear the talk.'

'That is a old, old one,' Galahad say. 'So this is the underground train I hear so much about?'

'Yes,' Moses say. Moses make up his mind to treat Galahad in a special way because he behaving as if he think he back home in Port of Spain or something. Still, he had to admit that it look as if Galahad have a lot of guts, the way how he getting on, the way how he land without any luggage, and Moses still amaze how he standing the cold without no winter clothes.

Galahad say: 'I find the train stopping often. Why is that?'

'Ask London Transport,' Moses say.

'Which part you living?' Galahad say.

'In the Water. Bayswater to you until you living in the city for at least two years.'

'Why they call it Bayswater? Is a bay? It have water?'

'Take it easy,' Moses say. 'You can't learn everything the first day you land. And you might notice we don't talk much in the tube because it making too much noise and you have to raise your voice.'

'How fast we going?'

'If you must talk tell me about Frank,' Moses say. 'He get married yet? It had a girl in St James used to write him every week when he was up here.'

When they get to the Water Galahad want to stand up and look at everything, though it ain't have anything to look at, but Moses hurry him home because the fog like it getting thicker and it making cold too bad.

Sir Galahad look around in Moses room.

'You have a small room, man,' he say.

'You will get a better one for yourself,' Moses say.

'What is that in the corner?'

'A gas fire. I better put it on. You have a shilling change on you?' Moses have shilling, but he have a feeling that if he don't tap the Galahad early he would never be able to do it later on.

Galahad hand Moses a shilling and watch him put it in the slot in the meter and light the gas.

First thing Galahad say is: 'You can't put in a piece of lead shape like a shilling instead? Frank say he used to do that.'

'Take it easy,' Moses say, 'all these questions you asking is good questions, but you will find out for yourself before long.'

'That small fire does keep the room warm?'

'Yes,' Moses say, 'but if I get the room I expect upstairs you could stay here and you wouldn't need to put it on, seeing that winter is like high noon to you.'

Moses heat up a pot of rice and peas and they eat. Moses keeping quiet because he don't want to crank up the old Galahad who look as if he like to talk a lot. But when they finish eating he get in a better mood and he decide to make the position clear.

'Listen,' he say, 'you can stay here tonight—you will have to sleep on them two chairs. But tomorrow, if the landlord don't agree for you to have this room, you will have to find a place. And also you have to look for work. I not saying you is a ants, but it have enough ants already in London. Though the boys does have to get up and hustle a lot, still every man on his own. It ain't have no s— over here like "both of we is Trinidadians and we must help out one another." You going to meet a lot of fellars from home who don't even want to talk to you, because they have matters on the mind. So the sooner you get settled the better for you. London not like Port of Spain. Don't ask plenty questions, and you will find out a lot. I don't usually talk to fellars like this, but I take a fancy for you, my blood take you. Tell me, what you used to do before you come?'

'I was working Point-a-Pierre in the oilfields,' Galahad say.

'Where you used to live?'

'Down south, San Fernando, in Mucurapo Street.'

'Eh-heh! You know Mahal?'

Mahal was a mad Indian fellar who used to go around town playing as if he driving car, putting in gear and stepping on the x and making hand signals and blowing horn.

'But how you mean? Everybody know Mahal!'

'He must be catching arse with the new type of gear it have on them cars now!' Moses laugh.

Galahad laugh. 'He still driving old-model.'

'And how about Palace Theatre? Is still there? Boy, when I was there the film used to burst every minute.'

'Yes man, the Palace still there, but they showing a set of Indian pictures now to make money.'

'I hear they build-over the market, is true?'

And old Moses start to get nostalgic now that he have a friend who just arrive from Trinidad, and the two of them talk a long time, until they feel sleepy.

Galahad put the two chair together and fall asleep right away. Moses watch him, and take a blanket off the bed and throw on him. But Galahad throw it back and ask Moses how he could sleep with blanket when it so hot.

'I think you best hads see a doctor tomorrow first thing,' Moses say. 'Something must be wrong with you.'

But Galahad was snoring already.

The next morning Moses get up about half-past nine and wash face and scrub teeth and comb hair, and still Galahad was sleeping, with a smile on his face.

Moses shake him rough. 'Get up man,' he say, 'is time to go and look for work. This is not a holiday camp.'

Galahad yawn and stretch. 'What you bending down so near the fire for and shivering like that?'

Moses glare. 'All right,' he say, 'don't over-play it, so you don't feel cold, so all right, take it easy.'

'I never thought my first morning in London would be like this,' Galahad say as he comb his hair.

'What you thought? That you would wake up in the Savoy?'

It have a kind of fellar who does never like people to think that they unaccustomed to anything, or that they are strangers in a place, or that they don't know where they going. They would never ask you how to get to Linden Gardens or if number 49 does go down High Street Ken. From the very beginning they out to give you the impression that they hep, that they on the ball, that nobody could tie them up.

Sir Galahad was a fellar like that, and he was trying hard to give Moses the feeling that everything all right, that he could take care of himself, that he don't want help for anything. So that same morning when they finish eating Moses tell him that he would go with him to help him find a work, but Galahad say: 'Don't worry man, I will make out for myself.'

'You don't know this place boy,' Moses say. 'Work not so easy to get as you think.'

'Don't worry with the old man,' Galahad say, 'he will take care of things.'

'Well,' Moses say, 'I must say you have guts, and perhaps you doing the best thing, for you can't learn no better way than by going around on your own. I could save you some trouble

by telling you where to go and where not to go, but I won't
bother. But take a little advice, old man. Go and see about a work
first, because supposing you get one far from the Water, it won't
make no sense to take this room, you will have to try and get
one near the work.'

Galahad know that Moses talking good talk, but he don't want
him to feel that he want any help from him. When he was
leaving Trinidad and Frank tell him a friend would meet him
at Waterloo, Galahad say why the hell you bother with that for?
But Frank tell him it all well and good to play boldface in a
small place like Trinidad, but when he land in London it would
be different, and he would be sure to need a friend there.

While Galahad sit there not saying anything Moses went on:
'Listen, I know fellars like you, you know. You try to fool
people that you know everything, then when you get lash you
come bawling.'

'All right mister London,' Galahad say, 'you been here for
a long time, what you would advice me as a newcomer to do?'

'I would advice you to hustle a passage back home to Trinidad
today,' Moses say, 'but I know you would never want to do
that. So what I will tell you is this: take it easy. It had a time
when I was first here, when it only had a few West Indians in
London, and things used to go good enough. These days, spades
all over the place, and every shipload is big news, and the
English people don't like the boys coming to England to work
and live.'

'Why is that?' Galahad ask.

'Well, as far as I could figure, they frighten that we get job
in front of them, though that does never happen. The other
thing is that they just don't like black people, and don't ask me
why, because that is a question that bigger brains than mine
trying to find out from way back.'

'Things as bad over here as in America?' Galahad ask.

'That is a point the boys always debating,' Moses say. 'Some
say yes, and some say no. The thing is, in America they don't

like you, and they tell you so straight, so that you know how you stand. Over here is the old English diplomacy: "thank you sir," and "how do you do" and that sort of thing. In America you see a sign telling you to keep off, but over here you don't see any, but when you go in the hotel or the restaurant they will politely tell you to haul—or else give you the cold treatment.'

'I know fellars like you,' Galahad say in turn. 'You all live in a place for some time and think you know all about it, and when any green fellars turn up you try to frighten them. If things bad like that how come you still holding on in Brit'n?'

'You don't believe, eh?' Moses say. 'Listen, I will give you the name of a place. It call Ipswich. There it have a restaurant run by a Pole call the Rendezvous Restaurant. Go there and see if they will serve you. And you know the hurtful part of it? The Pole who have that restaurant, he ain't have no more right in this country than we. In fact, we is British subjects and he is only a foreigner, we have more right than any people from the damn continent to live and work in this country, and enjoy what this country have, because is we who bleed to make this country prosperous.'

'Well look,' Galahad say, 'we could stay here talking all day, but I better go and look for work. Where you have to go to?'

'The employment exchange by Edgware Road. You will have a lot of company there, you shouldn't feel lonely. What work you used to do in the oilfields?'

'Electrician.'

'Well you better tell them that, else they will want to throw some hard work on you, lift iron and heavy box or something.'

'I did hear some fellars talking on the train when we was coming from Southampton, about how you could go on the dole if you ain't working, and how they intend to find out about it before they start to hustle.'

'It have some fellars like that,' Moses say. 'You want to be like that?'

Sir Galahad hesitate like if he thinking, then he say, 'No. If

I can't get electrician work I will take something else for the time being.'

'But you could refuse jobs, you know,' Moses press the Galahad, wanting to find out what kind of fellar he really is. 'And all the time the State will go on supporting you. By and by you will learn the ropes and how you could coast a long time without work.'

Galahad think about all the things that Moses tell him, then he say, 'Boy, I don't know about you, but I new in this country and I don't want to start antsing on the State unless I have to. Me, I am a born hustler.'

'I wish it had plenty other fellars like you,' Moses say, 'but a lot of parasites muddy the water for the boys, and these days when one spade do something wrong, they crying down the lot. So don't expect that they will treat you like anybody special—to them you will be just another one of them black Jamaicans who coming to London thinking that the streets paved with gold.'

'Something else I want to tell you,' Galahad say. 'I know you mean well telling me all these things, but papa, I want to find out for myself. So just tell me how to get to this place and I will go. You not working today?'

'I have a night work.'

'You didn't work last night.'

'I get the night off. But I have to go tonight. Anyway, I not leaving until late this evening, so you will meet me here when you come back. Now, go down the road until you come to Westbourne Grove, and there any bus going up towards Paddington—you better ask somebody—will take you to the school.'

With that, Moses start shining his shoes, and Sir Galahad went out to try and get a work.

Galahad make for the tube station when he left Moses, and he stand up there on Queensway watching everybody going about their business, and a feeling of loneliness and fright come on him all of a sudden. He forget all the brave words he was

talking to Moses, and he realise that here he is, in London, and
he ain't have money or work or place to sleep or any friend or
anything, and he standing up here by the tube station watching
people, and everybody look so busy he frighten to ask questions
from any of them. You think any of them bothering with what
going on in his mind? Or in anybody else mind but their own?
He see a test come and take a newspaper and put down the
money on a box—nobody there to watch the fellar and yet he
put the money down. What sort of thing is that? Galahad
wonder, they not afraid somebody thief the money?

He bounce up against a woman coming out the station but
she pass him like a full trolley before he could say sorry. Everybody doing something or going somewhere, is only he who
walking stupid.

On top of that, is one of those winter mornings when a kind
of fog hovering around. The sun shining, but Galahad never
see the sun look like how it looking now. No heat from it, it
just there in the sky like a force-ripe orange. When he look up,
the colour of the sky so desolate it make him more frighten. It
have a kind of melancholy aspect about the morning that making
him shiver. He have a feeling is about seven o'clock in the
evening: when he look at a clock on top a building he see is only
half-past ten in the morning.

By and by he drift down to Whiteleys. Suddenly he stand up
and look back. He wonder if he could find his way back to
Moses room! Jesus Christ, suppose he get lost? He ain't even
remember the name of the street where Moses living. In the
panic he start to pat pocket to make sure he have money on
him, and he begin to search for passport and some other papers
he had. A feeling come over him as if he lost everything he have
—clothes, shoes, hat—and he start to touch himself here and
there as if he in a daze.

Suddenly Galahad feel a hand on his shoulder and though he
want to look and see who it is, is as if the hand paralyse him
and he can't move. He just stand up there and he hear a voice

say: 'Move along now, don't block the pavement.'

When he was able to look Galahad see a policeman near him. Again he panic, though he ain't do anything against the law. Still is so people does feel in Trinidad when police near them, as if, even though they ain't commit a crime, the policeman would find something wrong that they do and want to lock them up.

Galahad start to stammer, all the big talk left him now.

'Can I help you to get some place?' the policeman say.

'I looking for the employment exchange,' Galahad say, looking around as if he expect it to be near.

'You have to catch a bus over there,' the policeman say, pointing across the road. 'The conductor will tell you where to get off.'

'Thanks,' Galahad say. He went across the road quick and stand up by Queen's to catch himself.

'You getting on like a damn fool,' he tell himself. 'What happen to you? All of a sudden like you gone stupid. Take it easy,' he say, unconsciously repeating Moses advice. 'You new in this place, it will take you some time to settle in.'

But the pep talk ain't do much to help, and he nearly dead with joy when he look up the road and see Moses coming. He start to whistle monkeyeric like how fellars in the West Indies whistle when they see a friend and want to attract attention. But he didn't have to do that, for Moses was coming straight to him.

'Moses,' he say, 'I too glad to see you, boy. If you don't mind I want you to come with me.'

'I thought so,' Moses say. 'Boy, you lucky I have soft heart, else you never see me again as long as you stay in London. You don't know that does happen? Fellars don't see one another for years here. Anyway, one thing is you must done with all this big talk.'

'Yes, yes,' Galahad say, so relieved to see Moses that he putting his hands on his shoulders like they is old pals.

'Come and catch a bus,' Moses say, and he take Galahad to

43

the bus queue. When the bus come, Galahad pushing in front
of the other people though Moses try to hold him back, and the
conductor say, ' 'Ere, you can't break the queue like that, mate.'
And Galahad had to stand up and watch all the people who was
there before him get on the bus, and a old lady look at him with
a loud tone in her eye, and a girl tell a fellar she was with:
'They'll have to learn to do better, you know.'

'I tell you to take it easy,' Moses say when they was in the bus,
'you not in Park Street waiting for a trolley.'

'Fares please.'

'Two fours,' Moses say, and he nudge Galahad. 'Pay.'

Galahad hand the conductor a pound because he not sure how
much two fours is.

When the conductor gone Moses say, 'You could always tell
when a test new in London—he always handing the conductor
pound note or ten-shilling cause he ain't learn yet how to work
out money in pounds, shillings and pence.'

'That was fourpence,' Galahad say to himself. 'That is four
pennies, and we pay eight. Eight twos are sixteen.' Aloud to
Moses: 'That was sixteen cents.'

'You sharp,' Moses say. 'Keep practising.'

When they get to the building that mark Ministry of Labour
Galahad see it had a lot of notice box with glass window on the
walls with all kind of vacancies for instrument repairers and
makers and turners and millers, and operators of this and that.
Sign like: Gateway to a Secure Future Join the Post Office as
a Postman hit him between the eyes, and a lot of others that encouraging you to join the army and the navy and the air force.

'Like plenty job going,' he tell Moses.

'Let we go inside,' Moses say. And when they was inside,
with a lot of other tests sitting around, Moses tell Galahad to go
to the desk that mark Enquiries and tell the clerk he want a
job.

The clerk take down some particulars and tell Galahad to

wait that they would call him, and he went and sit down with Moses.

After a while they call Galahad name and he went into a small cubicle where a test was sitting at a desk.

'What work can you do?' the clerk ask him.

'Electrician,' Galahad say.

'Electrician,' the clerk say to himself, and he look through some papers. 'We haven't got anything for you at the moment. Will you go to the next building and register and get your insurance card, please.'

Moses take him round the block to the next building. When they enter a kind of atmosphere hit Galahad hard so that he had to stand up against the wall for a minute. It ain't have no place in the world that exactly like a place where a lot of men get together to look for work and draw money from the Welfare State while they ain't working. Is a kind of place where hate and disgust and avarice and malice and sympathy and sorrow and pity all mix up. Is a place where everyone is your enemy and your friend. Even when you go to draw a little national assistance it don't be so bad, because when you reach that stage is because you touch bottom. But in the world today, a job is all the security a man have. A job mean place to sleep, food to eat, cigarette to smoke. And even though it have the Welfare State in the background, when a man out of work he like a fish out of water gasping for breath. It have some men, if they lose their job it like the world end, and when two-three weeks go by and they still ain't working, they get so desperate they would do anything.

'You see that fellar there?' Moses nod his head at a old English fellar rolling a cigarette. 'He is one of the regulars. He does only draw dole. The last time I was here was last year, and he still in the queue.'

Was a long room that Galahad see, shape like a L, and it have a counter going all the way, and on this counter it have files that in immediate use. It have some folding chairs at the beginning and the ending of the L, where some tests sit down waiting like guilty criminals. Over the counter it have numbers on placards 1, 2, 3, 4, and so on. Over the counter it also have a pipe what have the electric wires in it, and the clerks and them have pencils tie-up on the pipe with long string, dangling down to the counter, for the boys to sign up with. Fellars stand up in little groups here and there, all of them looking destitute and poor-me-one. It had a folding blind, and two fellars was getting in the folds to keep warm. The floor dirty with footprint and cigarette butt. The walls have plenty notice hang up, asking you to join the forces, and telling you what you must do to get pension and insurance and all that kind of thing.

'You see them papers it have on the counter?' Moses tell Galahad. 'One time in this office they used to have plenty more, but one day a Jamaican fellar come in and get ignorant and start to make rab. He tear up all the files and papers they had on the counter, and he make a snatch at one of the clerk behind. He bawling out and cursing and getting on like if he mad, and police had was to come and take him away. Since that time, the clerks not taking any chances, and the only files they have on the counter now is those that they using the same time.'

A few fellars call out to Moses, asking him what he doing in the school, if he on the dole, but Moses say no, he only showing a new test around.

'Now, on all the records of the boys, you will see mark on the top in red ink. J—A, Col. That mean you from Jamaica and you black. So that put the clerks in the know right away, you see. Suppose a vacancy come and they want to send a fellar, first they will find out if the firm want coloured fellars before they send you. That save a lot of time and bother, you see. In the beginning it cause a lot of trouble when fellars went saying that they come from the labour office and the people send them away saying it ain't have no vacancy. They don't tell you outright that they don't want coloured fellars, they just say sorry the vacancy get filled. But this office here ain't so bad, some of the clerks — up, but on the whole they treat you decent.'

And so between Moses and the labour office Galahad get fix up. When they was outside and Galahad showing him the unemployment card, Moses say, 'Keep that careful, and don't go about the place making grandcharge when you ain't have work. One time a fellar was trying to impress some girls in a café, talking all kind of big talk and saying how he have a big work in the government service. Same time he put his hand in his pocket to take out something and the unemployment card drop out.'

'You think I will get a work?' Galahad ask.

'Sure. When you come back to report tell them you will take anything for the time being. And now, we better go and see the landlord about the room.'

* * *

When Moses did arrive fresh in London, he look around for a place where he wouldn't have to spend much money, where he could get plenty food, and where he could meet the boys and coast a old talk to pass the time away—for this city powerfully lonely when you on your own.

It had such a place, a hostel, and you could say that in a way most of the boys graduate from there before they branch off on their own and begin to live in London. This place had some genuine fellars who really studying profession, but it also had fellars who was only marking time and waiting to see what tomorrow would bring.

It had a big dining room, and you had was to buy a meal ticket before you could get any food. Well some of the boys soon get in with the servant girls and get meal tickets free. Sometimes in the evening some fellars coming in, watching in the queue to see if they see a friend who would buy them a meal. Then afterwards in the lounge they would sit around—the genuine fellars with text-books in they hand, and some fellars

47

with the *Worker*, and big discussion on politics and thing would start up. Especially with them who come from British Guiana and don't want federation in the West Indies, saying that they belong to the continent of South America and don't want to belittle themself with the small islands. Meanwhile a African fellar would be playing the piano—he would give you a classic by Chopin, then a calypso, then one of them funny African tune. It had a game them Africans used to play with a calabash shell and some seeds, and nobody but a African could understand it, and all the time two-three of them sitting by a table playing this game. In another room had a pingpong table, and they used to play knockout, and some sharp games used to play there. In another room had a billiards table.

Them was the old days, long before test like Galahad hit London. But that don't mean to say it didn't have characters. There was a fellar name Captain. Captain was Nigerian. His father send him to London to study law, but Captain went stupid when he arrive in the big city. He start to spend money wild on woman and cigarette (he not fussy about drink) and before long the old man stop sending allowance.

Cap had a greenstripe suit and a pair of suede shoes, and he live in them for some years. He used to wash the clothes every night before he go to sleep, and when he get up press them, so that though he wearing the same things they always fairly clean. If he have money, he would get up in the morning. If not, he would sleep all day, for to get up would mean hustling a meal. So all day long he stay there in bed, not really sleeping but closing his eyes in a kind of squint. Come evening, Cap get up, go in the bathroom and look to see if anybody leave a end of soap for him to bath with. Come back, press the clothes and put them on, comb hair, blow the nose in the sink and gargle loud, watch himself in the mirror, and then come down the stairs to the dining room, wiping his face with a clean white handkerchief.

The old Cap have the sort of voice that would melt butter in the winter, and he does speak like a gentleman. So the thing is, after he sponge on all the fellars he know for meals, he used to look around for newcomers, and put on a soft tone and the hardluck story.

It have some men in this world, they don't do nothing at all, and you feel that they would dead from starvation, but day after day you meeting them and they looking hale, they laughing and they talking as if they have a million dollars, and in truth it look as if they would not only live longer than you but they would dead happier.

Cap was a man like that. Cap had plenty work, but he only stay a few days at any of them. And though he never have money in his pocket, yet he would be there, there with the boys, having a finger in everything. Cap only smoking Benson and Hedges—if you offer him a Woods he would scorn you. If he manage to hustle a pound, he eating a big meal, belching, buying a pack of B and H, and he ready to face the world.

Come a time when the warden of the hostel tired hearing Cap talk about the allowance that coming and never come, and tell him he have to leave. As luck would have it, Cap was staying in the same room with Moses, and he tell Moses not to say anything, but he would go out during the day and sneak back in the room to sleep in the night.

One morning the warden get suspicious and he begin to make a rounds looking for Cap, and when he come to Moses room the old Cap get so frighten that he start to rattle. He fly out the bed and went down on his knees before Moses, clasping his hands as if he saying prayers.

'Don't say that I am here,' he beg Moses, 'I would get in trouble.' And he went and hide in the clothes closet.

The warden open the door and look around and ask Moses if anybody else in the room, but he say no.

Captain come out after and start to shake Moses hand and thank him.

'You will have to go,' Moses say. But though he threaten the

Captain often, Cap still hanging out in Moses room in the hostel.

To make things worse, he start getting up in the night and saying that he see a white pigeon flying over his bed.

'It ain't have no pigeon in here,' Moses say.

'But I tell you I saw it!' Cap drawing back under the blankets. 'It must be the spirit of my father from Nigeria.'

Another night Cap wake Moses up. 'Believe me, I saw an angel with a harp playing over your bed,' he tell Moses.

'Listen,' Moses say. 'The next time you see that angel playing a —ing harp over my bed, you don't say or do anything. I like harp music, and he come to inspire me.'

One time Cap make a hundred pound. He hear that some English fellars who want car used to get Africans to buy them, saying they leaving the country. In that way they get away from a big set of purchase tax. Then the African would use the car a bit and sell it to the fellar who finance the venture as second-hand car. The Cap get in this racket, and make a hundred pound, but it went through his hands so quick that the morning he wake up broke he was surprise.

Things reach a head at the hostel and he had to pull out. Cap walk out as if he going for a stroll, with a toothbrush in his pocket. Brazen as ever, he went to a hotel and put on the soft tone, explaining he was a student and expected his allowance any day. Cap face so innocent that the clerk start calling him 'mister' and hustle to get him a room. No cheap room, one of the best, and Cap insisting on the ground floor too.

One thing with Cap, he love woman too bad. He is one of them fellars who would do anything to get a woman, and it ain't have a night that he not coasting down the Bayswater Road, or drifting round by the Circus. In fact, all the odd money that he need he get from women that he pick up here and there about the place. So what he doing is sleep in the day, and go out in the night to look for cat and sponge a meal whenever he could.

Well of course the hotel people begin to get uneasy when two weeks go by and Captain allowance ain't come, and they tell him he would have to leave. So Cap went out for a walk and didn't come back. In the Water, it hardly have a place where he ain't do the same thing, from boarding house to hotel, from room to room. He had to widen the area after a time. One day you would hear he living Caledonia, another time he move to Clapham Common, next time you see him he living Shepherd's Bush. Week after week, as landlord and landlady catch up with him, the Captain moving, the wandering Nigerian, man of mystery. Nobody could contact Cap, is only by chance you bouncing him up here and there about London.

'Where you living now Cap?'

A kind of baby smile, and 'Victoria.'

'Ah,' Moses tell Galahad when he was giving him ballad about Cap, 'is fellars like that who muddy the water for a lot of us. You see how it is? One worthless fellar go around making bad, and give the wrong impression for all the rest.'

Cap had an Austrian girl who was a sharp dresser, all kind of fur coat in the winter, and in the summer some kind of dress that making fellars whistle and turn round. As long as Cap had a place to take she, where have a bed to relax, this Austrian was all right. And for Cap, he used to take she round by all the fellars he know when he ain't have no place to stay himself.

This kind of life going on, and the Austrian trying she best to make Cap look for work.

'Why don't you get a job,' she tell Cap, 'there are many jobs around, and all your friends are working.'

'Jobs are hard to get,' Cap say cagey, 'it is not as easy as you think. I have tried many times.'

On one of those many times, the employment exchange send Cap to a railway to get a storekeeping work for seven pounds. When Cap go, the fellar in charge look at him and say yes, it have a work, but is not storekeeping work, and the pay is six ten.

'What kind of work it is?' Cap say. At this stage in his acquaintance with the boys he does forget proper English and many times you would mistake him for a West Indian, he get so hep.

The fellar take Cap to the back of the station, and behind there real grim. The people who living in London don't really know how behind them railway station does be so desolate and discouraging. It like another world. All Cap seeing is railway line and big junk of iron all about the yard, and some thick, heavy cable lying around. It have some snow on the ground, and the old fog at home as usual. It look like hell, and Cap back away when he see it.

'They tell me the pay was seven pounds,' Cap say, backing back.

'They made a mistake,' the fellar say. 'Do you think you can shift that piece of cable?'

'Take it easy,' Cap say.

'Go on, have a try,' the fellar urge.

'Take it easy,' Cap say. 'I will think about it and let you know.'

When he meet Moses he tell him how they was threatening him with this work in the railway.

'Is so it is,' Moses say. 'They send you for a storekeeper work and they want to put you in the yard to lift heavy iron. They think that is all we good for, and this time they keeping all the soft clerical jobs for them white fellars.'

Cap evade work so much that the Austrian start to get vex with him.

'How is it,' she tell Cap, 'that Moses has a job and manages on his salary? Why can't you get a job at the factory where he works?'

She nag Cap so much that at last Cap went to see Moses. He come back and tell the girl yes, he get a night-work same as Moses, and he would be starting right away.

In the night the Austrian come to the tube station with Moses and the Cap, and she buy a platform ticket and went down the platform with them, and she kiss Cap and wish him luck, and

Cap and Moses get on the train and went.

When the train reach Notting Hill Gate Cap get off and went to hustle woman as usual.

He do that for a week and the Austrian please that he working so hard. When Friday come she ask Cap how much pay he get.

'This is a place,' Cap say, 'where they don't pay you the first week that you work.'

The second week Cap carry on as usual, catching the tube in the Water and hopping off at the Gate.

When the week over Cap tell the girl that he left the work because it too hard.

How it is, that it have women, no matter how bad a man is, they would still hold on to him and love him? Though the Austrian find out what Cap was doing, she still stay with him. In fact, when things hard she start pawning wristwatch, ring, coat, shoes and anything to get a penny, and she giving Cap all the money. Cap used to send she round by a fellar name Daniel to borrow, and she would go there and cry big water and say how things hard, and the old Daniel, who can't bear to see a woman cry, would lend she five-six pounds.

When Daniel see she later and ask for the money, she say she give Cap to give him. When he ask Cap, Cap say he give the Austrian to give him.

One time Cap was in a thing with two woman. One was a German and the other was English. He borrow eight pounds from the frauline, and as time went by and she can't see him at all, she send the Chelsea police after him. Now Cap have a genuine fear of the law—though he might be the most shiftless and laziest fellar in London, one thing is that he never in any trouble with the law. So when the Chelsea police take after him he was frighten like hell.

Same time, he was in another thing with the English one. She spend some time in Africa and she know a lot of the boys from there. When she was in London she had a big work with a

respectable firm, and she always travelling light—toothbrush and
toothpaste and soap and towel and night things in a small
travelling bag, and after work she going round by one of the
fellars she know.

Well Cap get in with this thing, and when the German close
in on him, he take a wristwatch off the English girl and pawn
it and pay the frauline the eight pounds.

One night Cap take the English round by Daniel, and soon
after that Daniel was carrying the girl to ballet and theatre
and cinema. The English was smart—Cap not taking her anywhere or spending any money, while this Daniel taking she to
all the latest shows. Teahouse of the August Moon and Sadlers
Wells and to restaurants in the Circus and in Soho. So the
outcome was that she left Cap and begin to go with Daniel.

One night she tell Daniel how Cap take she wristwatch and
didn't give it back.

'What!' Daniel say, feeling like a knight rescuing a damsel in
distress, 'we have to do something about that!'

He and the girl went to Earl's Court, which part Cap had a
room at the time. When Daniel ask the landlady for Cap, she
say she don't know where he is, that he went away owing ten
pounds rent.

Somewhere in London Cap hear the rumour that Daniel looking for him, so he went to Daniel house one night, where he
meet the English girl.

'Cap,' Daniel say, 'how you could do a thing like this, man?
You take the girl wristwatch and pawn it! You have to get it
back for she right away!'

Cap see he can't get out of the situation no how so he start
to buse the English girl, calling she all kind of whore and pros-
titute, saying how she could go with Daniel. And with that he
went away not to see Daniel again until the matter was forgotten.

One powerful winter Cap was shivering with cold, and the
sight touch Moses heart. He lend Cap a camelhair coat. When
spring come, Moses looking all about for Cap to get back the

coat. But he can't see Cap nowhere. Truth is it always happen that Cap see him first and hop off the bus or tube and run to hide. At last Moses run him to earth in Marble Arch one evening.

'Aye, you bitch,' Moses say, 'I looking for you all about. Where my coat?'

'I ain't have it, Moses,' Cap say in the baby voice.

'You best hads get it for me,' Moses say, 'or I set the police after you. I ain't fooling, man.'

At mention of police Cap turn white, which is a hell of a thing to see. And the next day he pass round by Moses house and drop the coat.

And yet when things real desperate with Cap is Moses self who helping him out. The Austrian used to complain to him about Cap. 'All day he is sleeping, sleeping, I do not know what to do.'

Moses say: 'Listen, I telling you, that man no good for you, he is a worthless fellar who won't do no work, he would sleep with you and then look for somebody else to sleep with two minutes after, why you don't leave him?'

The Austrian ups and went back and tell Captain all what Moses say, and he and Cap had a big quarrel about it.

But still Moses have compassion on him. Round about that time the Captain trousers start to give way under the stress and strain of the seasons, and it was Moses who give him a old pair of pants. Moses couldn't help: everytime he going out with the Cap, Cap walking a little bit in front and asking him: 'See if my backside is showing, boy, this pair of trousers wearing thin.' And he look and see that Cap really in a bad way, and the soft heart was touched once more.

So Cap get a pair of cordurovs, and the Austrian girl give him a black blazer jacket.

One night something happen with Cap and Moses nearly go mad laughing when he find out afterwards, because at the time he didn't know nothing. He and Cap uses to coast Bayswater

Road, from the Arch to the Gate, nearly every night. Well it had one woman used to be hustling there, dress up nice, wearing fur coat, and every time when the boys pass she saying 'Bon soir,' in a hoarse voice, and the boys answering politely 'Bon soir' and walking on. But on this particular night things was scarce on the patrol and the old Cap thirst bad, so Moses tell him why he don't broach this big woman who always telling them 'Bon soir.'

Cap broach and he take the woman down by Gloucester Road and he was so hurry he couldn't wait but had was to begin as soon as she turn off the lights in the room.

Couple nights after they was talking to some women near a pub, when one of them turn to Captain and say: 'It was you who slept with that man the other night!'

And when the mark burst, Moses get to understand that this 'Bon soir' woman was really a test who used to dress up like a woman and patrol the area.

Moses start one set of laughing, and the old Cap laugh too. He tell Moses he didn't know anything until he begin, when he find the going difficult and realise that something wrong.

Since that time all the boys greeting Captain: 'Bon soir.'

Who can tell what was the vap that hit Cap and make him get married? A man like he, who ain't have nothing, no clothes, no work, no house to live in, no place to go? Yet is so things does happen in life. You work things out in your own mind to a kind of pattern, in a sort of sequence, and one day bam! something happen to throw everything out of gear, what you expect to happen never happen, what you don't expect to happen always happen, and you have to start thinking all over again.

Cap was a fellar like that—a fellar that you never know what he will be doing, which part he will be, what he will say. If you hear that Cap is Prime Minister of England, don't be surprised. If you hear that Cap kill four-five people in the Circus, don't be surprised. If you hear that Cap join a order of the monks and go to Tibet to meditate, be unconcerned.

Cap had a friend in Brighton who had a garage business, who was friending with a French girl. The French girl went back to France and tell she sister how things rosy in Brit'n, and the sister come, and Cap get in with she. This number was a sharp thing and Cap like it more than the regular Austrian. He tell Frenchy how the garage business not doing so well—this time so he give her the impression that he have part ownership in his friend business—and that he would be leaving it and taking up a post with the Nigerian Government. He tell the girl is a better job, and she believe every word he say, partly because his face so innocent, and partly because she can't understand English so well.

So thinking they would soon be off to Nigeria, the girl decide to marry Cap. She went to a vicar and give three weeks notice, and when the time come Cap went, wearing the corduroy trousers and the black blazer jacket and the suede shoes, which was still carrying him around. Them suede shoes, the makers would pay Cap a lot of money if they could get him to advertise how long they last him.

Without a cent in the world, no prospects, nothing at all Cap went to say 'I do.' When the vicar say they have to have a witness Cap run out on the road and was lucky to see a African fellar passing. He explain the position and the fellar say all right, but after the ceremony, when the vicar tell the fellar that he have to sign a book, the test shake his head.

'I not signing anything,' he say. 'I come to witness, and I witness. But I not signing anything.'

All the vicar explain to the test that it was necessary for the witness to sign the registry, the fellar decide that he not putting his name to any paper, and he went away.

Good thing, the vicar wife was in, and she said she would witness.

Cap, not having any address at the time, give Frenchy Daniel address and left the girl, saying he have some business to attend to.

That evening when Daniel come home from work the landlord meet him by the door and say: 'Your wife has come.'

'My wife?' Daniel say, standing up stupid.

'Yes. She is waiting for you in your room.'

When Daniel hear that he fly up the steps to see who it was. He see Frenchy sitting there with all her luggage, waiting on the Captain. She manage to explain to Daniel what she was doing there, and now Daniel in a quandary. He don't know which part to find the Captain. At last he had to leave the girl and go to look, and he decide to try a allnight cafe in the Gate where Cap does always hang out, coasting lime over a cuppa or a cup of coffee, sitting there eyeing every woman, trying to make contact.

As luck would have it he spot the old Cap having a cuppa, sitting down on a stool like if he have all the time in the world and not a worry on his mind.

'Cap,' Daniel say, 'what the hell is this? Your wife home by me, man, with all she luggage.'

'Good lord,' Cap murmur, sipping tea and wiping his face with the clean white handkerchief. 'Good lord.'

'Don't just sit there and say good lord, man. Do something.'

'Look, Daniel, this is the way it is.' And Cap say how he have no place to take the wife.

'But Christ man why you get married if you have no place to live?'

'Good lord,' Cap murmur.

Now Cap gambling on Daniel thirst, so when they go back to the room Cap encouraging conversation and getting Frenchy to talk familiar with Daniel, and sure enough the old Daniel had the kettle on to make a cup of tea.

So the night wearing on, and Cap ain't making no move to move, he only sitting down there wondering how to get out of the mooch he find himself in. As for Frenchy, she puzzle that

Cap only sitting there and wouldn't get up.

Cap put on the soft tone and ask Daniel to lend him eight pounds.

'Eight pounds!' Daniel say. 'What you think, money growing on tree?'

'I will give it back to you tomorrow,' Cap say, making the sign of the cross with his forefingers and kissing it, as he see the West Indian boys do.

Daniel hesitate a little, but he want to impress the French girl. Now he is a fellar that does take them woman to Covent Garden and Festival Hall, and them girl does have big times in them places, for all they accustom to is a pint of mild, the old fish and chips, and the one and six local. Many times Daniel go round by Moses saying how he take so and so to see ballet, and Moses tell him that them girls won't appreciate those things.

'I want them to feel good that we coloured fellars could take them to these places,' Daniel say, 'and we could appreciate even if they can't.'

'You spending your money bad,' Moses say. 'Them girls ain't worth it.'

But Daniel does feel good when he do things like that, it give him a big kick to know that one of the boys could take white girls to them places to listen to classics and see artistic ballet.

'You don't treat your women right,' he tell Moses, 'as long as you could get them in the yard you satisfy. You don't spend no money on them.'

'Why I must spend my money on them frowsy women?' Moses say.

So with Frenchy sitting there—and Cap giving the impression that anytime Daniel want a little thing with she it would be all right—he fork over the money.

Upon that Cap went out and hail a taxi and take the girl away to a seven-guinea room in a hotel.

And so Cap start the married life. He had to shift out of the hotel when the week was up, but the French girl was getting money from France every week, and they live on that for a long time. Every time she ask him when they going to Nigeria, Cap say he waiting on some papers from the Nigerian Embassy.

Meanwhile the Austrian hear that Cap have another girl, but she didn't know it was so serious. When she find out she went by Moses to moan, but he tell she to go to hell, because he did warn her about Cap.

Cap carrying on the same sort of life like when he was single. He there with the French girl in the night, and when she fall asleep he putting on clothes and going out to hustle just as he used to do before he get married. It don't make no difference to him at all. Eventually Frenchy had to get a work in a store, and nothing please him better. He sleeping all day while she out working, and going out in the night. He make she buy a radiogram and he get some of the latest bop records to keep him company, and now and again he having a little party in the room.

He had a way, every time Moses have a girl visitor, he dropping in and won't leave at all, sitting down there on the bed as if he waiting for Moses to give him a share. This thing happen so often that Moses get damn vex.

One evening when a girl was there the bell ring and Moses went and open the door. From the moment he see Cap he start to get on ignorant.

'Get out, get to hell out, man!' he say, and he push Cap in the road and shut the door.

Still, the Captain living. Day after day you will see him, doing nothing, having nothing, owing everybody, and yet he there with this innocent face, living on and on, smoking Benson and Hedges when things good, doing without a smoke when things bad. Who in this world think that work necessary? Who say that a man must have two pairs of shoes or two trousers or two jackets? Cap with woman left and right—he have a way, he does pick up something and take it home and when he finish and she ask for money, throw she out on the streets. He have a way, he would broach any girl who he see going around with one of the boys.

Yet day after day Cap still alive, defying all logic and reason and convention, living without working, smoking the best cigarettes, never without women.

Sometimes you does have to start thinking all over again when you feel you have things down the right way.

*   *   *

During them first days at the hostel, Moses really meet some characters. It had another fellar name Bartholomew. Bart was the sort of fellar who have a pound, and come downstairs for a meal, and he see a friend who broken, and the friend beg him for a meal, and Bart do without eating himself so he wouldn't have to change the pound and ease up the friend.

He used to tell the boys about a fellar who was a good friend to him, who would do anything for him, and he would do anything for the fellar. One evening the friend come when Bart was out and ask Moses to lend him five shillings, saying that Bart would fix up when he come. Because Bart talk so much about the friendship Moses didn't hesitate. When Bart come back, Moses ask him for the five shillings.

'Oh God man, you mean to say you give the man five shillings?'

'How you mean?' Moses say, 'ain't he is your good friend?'

'Yes, but five shillings is five shillings. Why you lend the man the money? That is five shillings, boy, five shillings!'

Moses never get the five shillings from Bart.

Bart have light skin. That is to say, he neither here nor there, though he more here than there. When he first hit Brit'n, like a lot of other brown-skin fellars who frighten for the lash, he go around telling everybody that he is a Latin-American, that he come from South America. Bart had ambition that always too big for him. He always talking about this party and that meeting that he attend in the West End or in Park Lane. He had some contacts, and he really used to go to some places, but all he could talk about when he come back was the amount of sandwich he eat, and how he drink whisky like water. Once he tell the boys he on a big project, and he used to stay upstairs in his room all the time, only coming down for meals and rushing back. He do that for a week and then stop, and nobody ever hear anything more about the project.

It have to be made clear to Bart, from the time he see you, that you don't want to borrow money from him. That is his big worry. When he see you right away he would start to get on cagey, on the lookout, but as soon as it clear that you don't want anything from him the old Bart open up like a water tap and start to tell you all what happening in town. He always saying he ain't have no money, afraid that somebody might want to borrow.

'You is a damn fool,' Moses tell him. 'If you have two hundred pounds in the bank, that is yours old man, yours, and nobody could make you lend them. That is your money, and if you don't want to lend, who could make you?'

'Man Moses I really telling you, I haven't any.'

About a week after he would come and say quietly, as if nothing happen: 'Boy, I send two hundred pound to Trinidad yesterday.'

'I thought you say you ain't have no money,' Moses say.

And Bart laugh kiff-kiff, as if the whole thing is a joke.

Only fellar who ever tap Bart was Cap, and that happen in the very early days. Cap broach Bart and ask him to lend two and six.

'Eh?' Bart say, playing as if he can't hear, and putting his hand on his ear and cocking it up

'I asked you to lend me two and six,' Cap say. (Cap would try to borrow from Mr Macmillan if he get the chance.)

'Eh? What you say?' Bart turn the other ear to Cap and cock it up. 'I can't hear well.'

'I ask you to lend me five shillings,' Cap say loudly.

'Come back by the two and six ear,' Bart say, turning his head again.

In the end Cap get the two and six, but that was the first and last time Bart ever lend money.

When Bart leave the hostel he get a clerical job and he hold on to it like if is gold, for he frighten if he have to go and work in factory—that is not for him at all. Many nights he think about how so many West Indians coming, and it give him more fear than it give the Englishman, for Bart frighten if they make things hard in Brit'n. If a fellar too black, Bart not companying him much, and he don't like to be found in the company of the boys, he always have an embarrass air when he with them in public, he does look around as much as to say: 'I here with these boys, but I not one of them, look at the colour of my skin.'

But a few door slam in Bart face, a few English people give him the old diplomacy, and Bart boil down and come like one of the boys.

Bart does go to the laundry, take off the jacket he have, put on the clean one and leave the dirty one to clean. He does wear some collar until you can't see them. Jacket threadbare, shirt have hole and button missing (some big safety pin keeping it together), some hole that have a little socks in them, and he wearing pyjamas for underwear—the only thing he have against the winter is that he have to buy extra clothing. It had a time when Bart train himself to live only on tea for weeks. He hustling a cuppa where he could: just a cuppa, that is all he asking for. He lose weight, he come thin as a rake. Whenever he meet the Captain by Moses at mealtime, Captain saying: 'What's the matter with you Bart? You look thin.' And Bart, who know that Cap living worse than him, would marvel that no ill effects showing on that test. 'How you does do it, tell me Cap?' Bart ask, and the old Cap would smile that enigmatic smile as if he have the secret of the world to hand.

When Bart go round by Moses Moses would say: 'Take a plate from the cupboard and hit a pigfoot and rice,' and though the way he say it is no invitation, Bart lost to all intonation of voice: sometimes when Moses say 'No' Bart does hear 'Yes.'

At last even the old Moses patience wear thin. 'Listen man, you only coming here and eating my food all the time. I wouldn't mind if now and then you bring a chicken or a piece of beef or even a little sugar or a bottle of milk. But you coming here and eating my rations too much. This thing must stop.'

'But man Moses how you mean? I only coming round to see you and talk.'

Fellars like Bart and Cap, you can't insult them, no matter how you try. If you tell Bart to get out he would look at you and laugh. If you tell Cap he is a nasty, low-minded son of a bitch, he would ask you why you don't put the kettle on the fire to make tea?

Like Cap, Bart moving from place to place week after week, though he paying rent, he too fraid to get in trouble in this country, and he not as brazen as Cap. One time in Camden Town Bart get a small room, and he fall sick and he nearly dead in that room. He get pale and had fever and he coughing like a bass drum. Moses went to see him. Bart lay down there on this bed like he dead: when he start to cough he scattering blanket and shaking up like a old engine.

'What happen to you Bart?' Moses say, sitting down on the end of the bed when it finish shaking.

'Oh God old man, is a week I sick now, and I send a message to you long time, is only today you come?'

'I couldn't come earlier, boy. What happen to you?'

'Moses, I am dying. I feel as if I will dead right now.' And Bart rattling some cough from deep down.

A English fellar wearing glasses come in the room with a cup of Oxo and give it to Bart and went back out.

'You see that fellar?' Bart say, 'if wasn't for him I dead already. He giving me Oxo regularly, and that keeping me alive.'

But fellars like Bart, ordinary death through illness not make for them. In a few days the old Bart was back in circulation.

Though Bart thirst for woman, he can't make a note with them, no matter how hard he try. So the time when he hold on to a English thing he hold on tight.

'Man, the girl always want to go theatre, and cinemas, and shows,' he complain to Moses. 'She does leave me broken.'

'Well,' Moses say, 'you want to play gentleman, and you have to pay for it.'

If you see Bart girl sitting in the tube with she legs crossed, reading the *Evening Standard* through rimless glasses, you wouldn't think she uses to hang out at the Paramount by Tottenham Court Road in the old days before the law clean up that joint. But if you tell Bart that he vex too bad, because he serious about this girl. In fact he going steady, and at last he tell Moses that he make up his mind to married this girl.

'You damn fool,' Moses say, 'is that you would married?'

'Mind what you say about my girl,' Bart say.

The girl tell Bart to come home and meet the folks and Bart went. The mother was friendly and she went in the kitchen to make tea, leaving Bart sitting down in the drawing room. He make himself comfortable and was just looking at a *Life* magazine when the girl father come in the room.

'You!' the father shouted, pointing a finger at Bart, 'you! What are you doing in my house? Get out! Get out this minute!'

The old Bart start to stutter about how he is a Latin-American but the girl father wouldn't give him chance.

'Get out! Get out, I say!' The father want to throw Bart out the house, because he don't want no curly-hair children in the family.

65

Bart had was to hustle from the white people house, and go mourning to the boys.

Still, for him girl so hard to get that he still meeting the number, frighten that he won't be able to get another. But one thing lead to another and she start to slack off the old Bart bit by bit. One day he was to meet she by a bus stop in Edgware Road. He take a bus and was going there, when he notice that a fellar was talking to she in the queue. Bart stay in the bus and get off at the next stop and begin to walk down the road slowly. When he get to the queue the fellar wasn't there.

He ask the girl if she was talking to anybody while she was waiting, and she say no. All that evening Bart cold, cold to the girl, frighten that she was making a date with this fellar, and he can't understand why it is that she say she wasn't talking to anybody.

'I did see you talking to a fellar in the queue,' Bart say at last.

'I can't remember,' the girl say vaguely. 'Somebody did ask me how to get to St Stephen Gardens, but he left after I told him.'

But Bart have a feeling, that she giving him the horn regularly when they not together.

Eventually the girl move from the place where she was living and Bart can't find her at all. He start to get frantic. He look all about, any time he see any of the boys: 'You see Beatrice anywhere?'

He must be comb the whole of London, looking in the millions of white faces walking down Oxford Street, peering into buses, taking tube ride on the Inner Circle just in the hope that he might see she. For weeks the old Bart hunt, until he become haggard and haunted.

Knowing that she like the night lights, at last Bart get a work at a club as a doorman, and now night after night he would be standing up there, hoping that one night Beatrice might come to lime by the club and he would see her again.

It have men like that in the world, too.

*   *   *

Things does have a way of fixing themselves, whether you worry or not. If you hustle, it will happen, if you don't hustle, it will still happen. Everybody living to dead, no matter what they doing while they living, in the end everybody dead.

Tolroy eventually get the family settle. He manage to get two double room at the house he staying in in Harrow Road, but Agnes and Lewis went in another room in a house not far away. Then Tolroy take Lewis to the factory and get a work for him. It wasn't so hard to do that, for the work is a hard work and mostly is spades they have working in the factory, paying lower wages than they would have to pay white fellars.

Lewis is another character that does put your thinking out of gear. Though he have sense, you would think he stupid, because he always asking questions, and anything you tell him he would believe. Before he married Agnes, Lewis had a girl name Mable who went to Venezuela and say she would send for him when she get fix up down there, as she had family living there. Lewis start packing suitcase the day after she leave, and every day he looking out for the letter that would tell him to come. One day a fellar who was in Venezuela tell Lewis that he see Mable living with a fellar while he was there.

'You lie,' Lewis say.

'If I lie I die,' the test say.

'Who it is?' Lewis say, and he want to take a plane and fly to Venezuela right away and kill the fellar.

In the factory, Lewis working on the same job with Moses—getting pot scourers ready for packing. The night Tolroy bring Lewis, he introduce him to Moses.

'This is my sister husband.'

'So what?' Moses say.

'Keep an eye on him,' Tolroy say.

'How the family?' Moses say, remembering Waterloo.

'Boy, I not worrying my head,' Tolroy say. 'The old lady get a work at Lyons washing dish, and Tanty staying home to mind the children and cook the food.'

Moses say: 'Your business good.'

Every night, Lewis telling Moses all kind of episodes that happen to him, and knowing that Moses is a man about London he asking him all sorts of stupid questions.

'Moses,' he say, 'you think is true that it have fellars does go round by you when you out working and — your wife?'

If you tell Lewis that the statue on top of Nelson column in Trafalgar Square is not Nelson at all but a fellar what name Napoleon, he would believe you, and if you tell him that it have lions and tigers in Oxford Circus, he would go to see them. So Moses giving him basket for so.

'How you mean,' Moses say. 'That is a regular thing in London. The wife leave the key under the milk bottle, and while you working out your tail in the factory, bags of fellars round by your house with the wife.'

Half hour later Lewis came back worried. 'You really think so, Moses? I have suspicions, you know.'

'I telling you,' Moses say ruthlessly. 'You think if I was married I would ever do night work? You don't know London, boy.'

And after another half hour, Lewis gone to the foreman and say he have headache, that he can't do any work, that he have to go home right away. And as soon as he get home he starting to beat up Agnes, though the poor girl don't know what for.

Every night Lewis have something on the mind, and he does plague out Moses with talk and questions.

'I know who it is, you know,' he say confidentially. 'Is a fellar who does pass round by the house with a motorcycle.'

Another night: 'I sure I see the fellar. He does drive a car.'

Well, two-three times when he beat up Agnes, she went and

stay by Tolroy house with Tanty and she mother, but in the end she always come back.

'Why you don't leave that man for good?' Tanty say. 'He always beating you for nothing. Why he beat you this time?'

'The same reason,' Agnes say. 'He say that I does encourage other men home while he out working, and I swear to God I never talk to another man.'

'Moses,' Lewis say one night, 'if you was in my position you wouldn't do the same thing?'

'No,' Moses say.

'Why?'

'Well you only suspect the wife, you don't know anything for sure. Listen, women in this country not like Jamaica, you know. They have rights over here, and they always shouting for something.'

'But you tell me when fellars have night work other fellars go round by the house when the wife alone.'

'But I didn't say that fellars does go round by your wife. My mouth ain't no Bible.'

Still Lewis worried and imagining all kinds of things happening to the wife while he hustling in the factory. At last he put on such a beating on Agnes that she left him for good. Lewis didn't know, he thought she gone by Tanty house for the usual cool-off and he didn't bother for two days. But when she didn't turn up he went to look for she.

'Where Agnes?' he ask Tanty. 'Tell she is all right, she could come home now.'

'Agnes not here,' Tanty say.

'Is all right, I tell you,' Lewis say. 'Tell she to forget all about it.'

'But I tell you Agnes not here,' Tanty say. 'What happen, you beat she again last night?'

'How you mean she ain't here?' Lewis say, and he looking all about in the room.

'Which part she gone?' he ask Tanty.

'I don't know,' Tanty say. 'She didn't come here at all. But if she left you she have a right to.'

'Where else she could go to but here?' Lewis ask.

'Don't ask me,' Tanty say, 'all I know is she not here. You best hads report it to the police station that she missing.' Lewis start to get frighten, it look like this time Agnes serious. From that minute he start to bite his finger nails, and he bite them so low that he never had finger nail again. He went by the police station in Harrow Road, and he tell the police that his wife missing. They take down particulars, but case like that so common, and it have so many people in London (though it would be easy to spot a spade) that chances look slim: they tell Lewis not to worry that she would turn up any time.

Days go by and Lewis can't see Agnes, and he biting his fingers. One morning he get a summons and he panic. Agnes charge him with assault. He fly round by Moses.

'What this mean?' he ask Moses.

'It mean that your wife bring you up,' Moses say, wondering why these sorts of things does always happen to him. 'You will have to go to court.'

'To court!' Lewis say. 'What you think they will do?'

'They will lock you up,' Moses say. 'It have a jail in Wormwood Scrubs.'

'It have she address here,' Lewis say. 'You think I should go there and see her?'

'If I was you,' Moses say, 'I wouldn't do that. I would sit down and write she a nice letter to soften she up before you go to court.'

'I really love that woman,' Lewis say. 'But she does make me too jealous.'

'You better write the letter,' Moses say.

'You have any writing paper Moses?'

'Look some on the table.'

'What to tell she?'

'Tell she you sorry,' Moses say. 'Tell she come back home and everything would be all right.'

'That is the usual thing I say,' Lewis take out a Biro pen and unscrew the cap. 'She might think I always saying that.'

'Well what you want me to tell you old man?' Moses say. He was tired and wanted to sleep as he had a hard night in the factory.

But Agnes never reply to Lewis letter, and in the end she left him and he never see she again. Lewis went by Moses to learn how to live bachelor. He ask Moses all sorts of funny questions, like how he does live alone, what he does do with dirty clothes, how to boil rice and peas. About a month after Agnes left him Lewis get in with a little thing and he forget all about married life.

*   *   *

'Tanty, you wasting too much coal on the fire,' Tolroy say.

'Boy, leave me alone. I am cold too bad.' Tanty put more coal on the fire.

'You only causing smog,' Tolroy say.

'Smog? What is that?'

'You don't read the papers?' Tolroy say. 'All that nasty fog it have outside today, and you pushing more smoke up the chimney. You killing people.'

'So how else to keep warm?' Tanty say. 'You think this is Jamaica? My hand blue. I went out just now and bring back eight pound of potato, and my fingers couldn't straighten out from holding the bag, I thought I catch a cramp, I hot some water quick and wash my hands.'

'Old people like you, you only come here to make life miserable,' Tolroy say. When Ma not there Tolroy used to take lag on Tanty left and right for coming to London.

'I did know that when old age come is so the children would scorn me,' Tanty say, she voice low because she tired raising it.

'What else to expect, oh Lord? I mind you from the time you was a little boy running about naked in the backstreet in Kingston, and this is all the gratitude and thanks I get. Is so life is. What else to expect oh Lord?'

'I tired hearing that tune,' Tolroy say. 'Every time I tell you anything you have to remind me that you mind me when I was a little boy. All right, you mind me, so what? What for you leave that warm place to come up here and freeze to death? I didn't send for you. I only send for Ma, and what happen? The whole blasted family come to give me grey hair before my time, as if I haven't got enough worries as it is. Listen, you better advice that Lewis that he better stop beating Agnes. Here is not Jamaica, you know.'

'Why you don't tell him yourself? You fraid him?'

'Who me? Is just that he won't listen to me. Now Agnes gone and every time he see me he asking me: "You know where Agnes gone?" London not like Kingston, you know. A man could get lost here easy, it have millions of people living here, and your friend could be living in London for years and you never see him.'

'If you have anything to tell Lewis tell him yourself.'

'But serious, Tanty, is which part Agnes gone at all? This is the first time she stay away so long. Lewis really love her, you know. He look real miserable. He don't do any work in the factory all night. Why you don't tell him where Agnes is?'

'Tell him where Agnes is! You wait, you will hear just now. Every time he beating the poor girl for nothing, though the Probation Officer warn him. You know what? Agnes going to bring him up for assault!'

'Bring him up for assault!'

'Yes, I advice her. That's the only way to stop him, the way he getting on.'

'And she say yes?'

'Yes, she say yes. So you just wait and see.'

'Well anyway is none of my business. Tanty, make some tea for me, I want to go out.'

'Why you don't stay home and sleep, you work all night.'

'I have to go out. Make haste.'

'You talking about warning Lewis, but let me warn you, I know where you going. You think I don't know you have a white girl. You better watch out and don't get in no trouble. I mind you from a little boy.'

'All right Tanty. But make the tea quick.'

'White girls,' Tanty grumble as she put the kettle on the fireplace fire, 'is that what sweeten up so many of you to come to London. Your own kind of girls not good enough now, is only white girls. I see Agnes bring a nice girl friend from Jamaica to see us, but you didn't even blink on she. White girls! Go on! They will catch up with you in this country!'

The place where Tolroy and the family living was off the Harrow Road, and the people in that area call the Working Class. Wherever in London that it have Working Class, there you will find a lot of spades. This is the real world, where men know what it is to hustle a pound to pay the rent when Friday come. The houses around here old and grey and weatherbeaten, the walls cracking like the last days of Pompeii, it ain't have no hot water, and in the whole street that Tolroy and them living in, none of the houses have bath. You had was to buy one of them big galvanise basin and boil the water and full it up, or else go to the public bath. Some of the houses still had gas light, which is to tell you how old they was. All the houses in a row in the street, on both sides, they build like one long house with walls separating them in parts, so your house jam-up between two neighbours: is so most of the houses is in London. The street does be always dirty except if rain fall. Sometimes a truck does come with a kind of revolving broom and some pipes letting out water, and the driver drive near the pavement, and water come out the pipes and the broom revolve, and so they sweep the road. It always have little children playing in the road, because they ain't have no other place to play. They does draw hopscotch blocks on the pavement, and other things, and some of the walls of the buildings have signs painted like Vote Labour and Down With the Tories. The bottom of the street, it had a sweet-shop, a bakery, a grocery, a butcher and a fish and chips. The top of the street, where it join the Harrow Road, it had all kind of thing—shop, store, butcher, greengrocer, trolley and bus stop. Up here on a Saturday plenty vendors used to be selling provisions near the pavements. It had a truck used to come one time with flowers to sell, and the fellars used to sell cheap, and the poor people buy tulip and daffodil to put in the dingy room they living in.

It have people living in London who don't know what happening in the room next to them, far more the street, or how other people living. London is a place like that. It divide up in little worlds, and you stay in the world you belong to and you don't know anything about what happening in the other ones except what you read in the papers. Them rich people who does live in Belgravia and Knightsbridge and up in Hampstead and them other plush places, they would never believe what it like in a grim place like Harrow Road or Notting Hill. Them people who have car, who going to theatre and ballet in the West End, who attending premiere with the royal family, they don't know nothing about hustling two pound of brussel sprout and half-pound potato, or queuing up for fish and chips in the smog. People don't talk about things like that again, they come to kind of accept that is so the world is, that it bound to have rich and poor, it bound to have some who live by the Grace and others who have plenty. That is all about it, nobody does go into detail. A poor man, a rich man. To stop one of them rich tests when they are going to a show in Leicester Square and ask them for a bob, they might give you, but if you want to talk about the conditions under which you living, they haven't time for that. They know all about that already. People get tired after a time with who poor and who rich and who catching arse and who well off, they don't care any more.

It have a kind of communal feeling with the Working Class and the spades, because when you poor things does level out, it don't have much up and down. A lot of the men get kill in war and leave widow behind, and it have bags of these old geezers who does be pottering about the Harrow Road like if they lost, a look in their eye as if the war happen unexpected and they still can't realise what happen to the old Brit'n. All over London you would see them, going shopping with a basket, or taking the dog for a walk in the park, where they will sit down on the bench in winter and summer. Or you might meet them hunch-up in a bus-queue, or waiting to get the fish and chips hot. On Friday or a Saturday night, they go in the pub and buy a big glass of mild and bitter, and sit down by a table near the fire and stay here coasting lime till the pub close. The old fellars do that too, and sometimes they walk up a street in a plush area with their cap in their hand, and sing in a high falsetto, looking up at the high windows, where the high and the mighty living, and now and then a window would open and somebody would throw down threepence or a tanner, and the old fellar have to watch it good else it roll in the road and get lost. Up in that fully furnished flat where the window open (rent bout ten or fifteen guineas, Lord) it must be have some woman that sleep late after a night at the Savoy or Dorchester, and she was laying under the warm quilt on the Simmons mattress, and she hear the test singing. No song or rhythm, just a sort of musical noise so nobody could say that he begging. And she must be just get up and throw a tanner out the window. Could be she had a nice night and she in a good mood, or could be, after the night's sleep, she thinking about life and the sound of that voice quavering in the cold outside touch the old heart. But if she have a thought at all, it never go further than to cause the window to open and the tanner to fall down. In fact when the woman throw the tanner from the window she didn't even look down: if a man was a mile away and he was controlling a loudspeaker in the street moving up and down, the tanner would have come the same way. Also, for the old test who singing, it ain't have no thought at all about where this tanner come from, or who throw it, man, woman or child, it ain't make no difference. All he know is that a tanner fall in the road, and he had to watch it else it roll and get lost.

When you come to think of it, everything in life like that. Maybe afterwards if a friend go to that woman and say that the test is a lazy fellar and worthless, she wouldn't throw any more money if he pass up that street. Or if the friend say he is a poor old man having a hard time she will throw a bob the next time he pass.

People in this world don't know how other people does affect their lives.

Or else, the old fellars go by the people that queuing up for the cinema. Not so much by the one and sixes and two and nines, but by the three and twos and four shillings. And some of them old fellars so brazen that though it against the law to beg they passing the old cap around, and if they see a policeman they begin to sing or play a old mouthorgan. What impulse does prompt people to give no one knows. Is never generosity—you could see some of them regret it as soon as they give. But is a kind of feeling of shame. One fellar give, and the others feel shame if they don't put a penny in the old man hat.

The grocery it had at the bottom of the street was like a shop in the West Indies. It had Brasso to shine brass, and you could get Blue for when you washing clothes, and the fellar selling pitchoil. He have the pitchoil in some big drum in the back of the shop in the yard, and you carry your tin and ask for a gallon, to put in the cheap oil burner. The shop also have wick, in case the wick in your burner go bad, and it have wood cut up in little bundles to start coal fire. Before Jamaicans start to invade Brit'n, it was a hell of a thing to pick up a piece of saltfish anywhere, or to get thing like pepper sauce or dasheen or even garlic. It had a continental shop in one of the back streets

in Soho, and that was the only place in the whole of London
that you could have pick up a piece of fish. But now, papa!
Shop all about start to take in stocks of foodstuffs what West
Indians like, and today is no trouble at all to get saltfish and rice
This test who had the grocery, from the time spades start to
settle in the district, he find out what sort of things they like to
eat, and he stock up with a lot of things like blackeye peas and
red beans and pepper sauce, and tinned breadfruit and ochro
and smoke herring, and as long as the spades spending money he
don't care, in fact is big encouragement, 'Good morning sir,' and
'What can I do for you today, sir,' and 'Do come again.'

All over London have places like that now. It have tailor shop
in the East End, near Aldgate Station, what owned by a cockney
Jew fellar. Well papa, when you go there on a Saturday you can't
find place to stand up, because the place full up with spades, and
the Jew passing round cigars free to everybody. (Cigars is on
Saturday, if you lime during the week he give you cigarettes.)
Is a small shop, and on the walls have photo of all the black
boxers in the world, and photo of any presentation or function
what have spades in it.

'Friend,' the Jew say, lighting up the cigar, 'when I make a
suit and you go to the West End, people stand back and look at
you. If I do anything you don't like, bring it back and I will fix
it immediately. If you still do not like my work, I will refund
your money. Who told you about this place, my friend?'

'A fellar I know.'

'Ah! Yes, I do a lot of business with you boys, and guarantee
complete satisfaction. Have another cigar to smoke later.' And
the test pulling cigar from all about and passing round to the
boys.

This time so the assistant measuring up with tape, asking who
want tight bottoms and loop in the waist for belt, and pulling
down all kind of Cromby from the shelf to show the boys. By the
time you ready to leave the shop the fellar have you feeling like

a lord even if you ain't give an order for a suit and you have him down one cigar.

'Come again, my friend,' he say as he give you another cigar for the road, and with the other hand he pull out a card from the top jacket pocket and hand you. 'Here is my card, and there is the telephone number. Open the door Jack,' and if the assistant too busy he himself hustling to open the door for you.

Another Jew fellar in Edgware Road does come out on the pavement when you looking in the show-window and hold your elbow and push you in the shop, whether you want anything or not. But he too cagey: once he make a cheap garbadeen suit for a Jamaican and hit him twenty-five guineas, and since that time the boys give the shop a long walk. This fellar also used to put cloth in the window with a certain price, and when you go inside the price gone up couple guineas.

Well Tanty used to shop in this grocery every Saturday morning. It does be like a jam-session there when all the spade housewives go to buy, and Tanty in the lead. They getting on just as if they in the market-place back home: 'Yes child, as I was telling you, she did lose the baby ... half-pound saltfish please, the dry codfish ... yes, as I was telling you ... and two pounds rice, please, and half-pound red beans, no, not that one, that one in the bag in the corner...'

All poor Lewis business talk out in that shop with Tanty big mouth, for it ain't have no woman like stand up and talk other people business like Tanty, and it didn't take she long to make friend and enemy with everybody in the district. She too like the shop, and the chance to meet them other women and gossip. She become a familiar figure to everybody, and even the English people calling she Tanty. It was Tanty who cause the shop-keeper to give people credit.

It had a big picture hang up on the wall of the shop, with two fellars in it. One is Mr Credit, and he surrounded with unpaid bills and he thin and worried, with his hand propping up his head. The other is Mr Cash, and he have on waistcoat with gold chain and he have a big belly and he laughing and looking prosperous. Tanty used to look at the picture and suck she teeth. One day she ask the shopkeeper if he don't know about trust.

'Trust?' the shopkeeper say.

'Yes,' Tanty say. 'Where I come from you take what you want and you pay every Friday.'

'Oh, credit,' the shopkeeper say, as if he please that he understand Tanty. 'We don't do business like that in this shop.' And he point to the picture on the wall.

'But you should,' Tanty say. 'We is poor people and we don't always have money to buy.'

Tanty keep behind the shopkeeper to trust, but he only smile when she tell him. Then one day Tanty buy a set of message and put it in she bag and tell him: 'You see that exercise books you have in the glasscase? Take one out and put my name in it and keep it under the counter with how much I owe you. Mark the things I take and I will pay you on Friday please God.'

And Tanty walk out the white people shop brazen as ever. When the Friday come, she pay what she owe

'I will only give you credit,' the shopkeeper say, to humour Tanty, but before long she spread the ballad all about that anybody could trust if they want, and the fellar get a list of creditors on his hands. However, every Friday evening religiously they all paying up, and as business going on all right he decide to give in. He take down the picture and put up one of the coronation of the Queen.

Everybody in the district get to know Tanty so well that she doing as she like. You know how them greengrocers and barrow boys don't want you to touch their goods at all because they put all the good things in front to make show and behind, from where they selling, they give all the rotten and bad ones. With Tanty it ain't have none of that.

'I want that cabbage,' Tanty does say, and pull a big one out from in front, and all the others it was propping up fall down.

'No no, give me tomatoes from in front,' she say, when fellars taking rotten ones from behind to sell. If anybody else get on so, even English people, is big trouble, but with Tanty is all right. She try to spread the credit business on the Harrow Road, but them proprietors was different than the fellar in the back street.

In them bakeries in London, if you buy a bread they does hand it to you just like that, without wrapping it in paper or anything. But not Tanty.

'Where I come from,' Tanty tell the bakery people, 'they don't hand you bread like that. You better put it in a paper bag for me, please.'

She used to get in big oldtalk with the attendants, paying no mind to people waiting in the queue.

'If I know Montego Bay!' she say. 'Why, I was born there, when I was a little girl I used to bathe in the sea where all those filmstars does go. If we does have a winter there? Well no, but it does be cold sometimes in the evening. Not like this cold! Lord, I never thought in my old age I would land up in a country like this, where you can't see where you going and it so cold you have to light fire to keep warm! Why I come to London? Is a long story, child, it would take up too much time, and people standing in the queue waiting. But I mind my nephew from the time he was a little boy, and he there here in London, he have a work in a factory...'

Like how some people live in small village and never go to the city, so Tanty settle down in the Harrow Road in the Working Class area. When Ma come home from work she used to ask about the outside world and Ma would tell she about tube train and Piccadilly Circus, and how the life so busy that if you don't watch out a car knock you down and you dead in the road.

'Why you don't take a tube and go and see the big stores it have in Oxford Street,' Ma say, but Tanty shake her head.

'I too old for that now,' she say, 'it don't matter to me, I will stay here by the Harrow Road.'

But all the same it rankle Tanty that she never travel in

tube or bus in London, and she make up she mind secretly to go if she get the chance and she have a good reason.

Ma had this work at a Lyons Corner House, and she had to go out early every morning and come back late in the evening. She wash cup and spoon and dish and glass for five pounds a week. Ma work in the back, in the kitchen, but she was near enough to the front to see what happening outside of the kitchen. She get to know the regular faces, and she get to know cup and dirty dish and spoon like she never know before. All the wares used to come from a square hole where the attendants push them. Only from the washing up Ma form a idea of the population of London: 'I never see so much dirty wares in my life,' she tell Tanty, 'it does have mountains of washing coming in. Where all these people come from?'

Sometimes in the evening Ma go to see Agnes, but mostly she and Tanty sit down before the fire knitting and talking about Jamaica.

Well one morning Ma forget and went to work with the key to open the cupboard what have all the rations in it, and Tanty didn't know what to do. Tolroy was out, and the children was spending time by Agnes, and she alone in the house. She try to pick the lock but is one of them Yale lock and she couldn't manage. Tanty was waiting for a good excuse to travel out of the district, and she decide to brave London and go to this place where Ma working to get the keys.

She put on the old fireman coat that Tolroy did get for her, and she tie a piece of coloured cloth on her head, and she went out to the Harrow Road. Tanty did hear how everybody saying that if you want to find out something you must ask a policeman, so though she see plenty people that she could ask she ignore them and look for a policeman. She didn't see one till she reach by the Prince of Wales.

'You could tell me where Greatport Street is, please,' Tanty say.

The policeman look at her close and say: 'Where?'

'Greatport Street,' Tanty say.

The policeman scratch his head. 'Are you sure of the name?'

'Something like that,' Tanty say, sure that the policeman would know.

'You don't mean Great Portland Street?' he say.

'Yes, that is it!' Tanty say. 'I thought it had a "land" in it.'

'The number 18B bus goes there,' the policeman say. 'The conductor will tell you where to get off.'

'I don't like these buses it have in London,' Tanty say. 'They too tall, I feel as if they would capsize. What about the tube train?'

'You could walk down to Westbourne Park Station,' the policeman say smiling.

'I won't have to change?' Tanty ask, getting frighten now at the idea.

'No, I don't think so.'

'Thank you very much,' Tanty say.

Though Tanty never went on the tube, she was like those people who feel familiar with a thing just by reading about it and hearing about it. Everybody does talk about the tubes and take them for granted, and even Tanty with she big mouth does have something to say: 'How you come? By tube? You travel on the Bakerloo Line? And you change to the Central at Tottenham Court Road? But I thought it was the Metropolitan Line that does pass there!'

But was plenty different when she find sheself in the station, and the idea of going under the ground in this train nearly make she turn back. But the thought that she would never be able to say she went made her carry on.

Eventually Tanty did get to the place where Ma working after asking questions all the way. She went straight into the place, and she peep through the square hole and she see Ma washing dish.

'Ma,' she call out, 'you had me in one set of confusion this morning. You left with the key to the cupboard and it ain't have nothing to cook.'

'Come round here in the back,' Ma say, frighten that Tanty stand up there talking so loud, and all the customers looking at she.

'No child,' Tanty say. 'Just give me the key and I will go, you best do the white people work and don't stop.'

Ma come and give Tanty the key, and ask she how she get to the place.

'I come by tube,' Tanty say cool, as if she travelling every day. 'How else you think? But I going back by bus.'

'Stay and eat a food as you here already,' Ma say.

'What!' Tanty say, 'eat this English food when I have peas and rice waiting home to cook? You must be mad! But don't let me keep you from your work.'

And Tanty went away, feeling good that she make the trip from Harrow Road at last.

'I hope this bus don't turn over,' she tell the conductor, because it didn't have room below and she had to go upstairs.

She was so frighten that she didn't bother to look out of the window and see anything, and when she get off at the Prince of Wales she feel relieved. Now nobody could tell she that she ain't travel by bus and tube in London.

*　　*　　*

When that first London summer hit Galahad he begin to feel so cold that he had to get a overcoat. Moses laugh like hell. 'You thought you get away from the weather, eh?' he say. 'You warm in the winter and cold in the summer, eh? Well is my turn now to put on my light suit and cruise about.'

'I don't know why I hot in the winter and cold in the summer,' Galahad say, shivering.

But for all that, he getting on well in the city. He had a way, whenever he talking with the boys, he using the names of the places like they mean big romance, as if to say 'I was in Oxford Street' have more prestige than if he just say 'I was up the road.' And once he had a date with a frauline, and he make a big point of saying he was meeting she by Charing Cross, because just to say 'Charing Cross' have a lot of romance in it, he remember it had a song called 'Roseann of Charing Cross.' So this is how he getting on to Moses:

'I meeting that piece of skin tonight, you know.' And then, as if it not very important, 'She waiting for me by Charing Cross Station.'

Jesus Christ, when he say 'Charing Cross,' when he realise that is he, Sir Galahad, who going there, near that place that everybody in the world know about (it even have the name in the dictionary) he feel like a new man. It didn't matter about the woman he going to meet, just to say he was going there made him feel big and important, and even if he was just going to coast a lime, to stand up and watch the white people, still, it would have been something.

The same way with the big clock they have in Piccadilly Tube Station, what does tell the time of places all over the world. The time when he had a date with Daisy he tell her to meet him there.

'How you don't know where it is?' he say when she tell him she don't know where it is. 'Is a place that everybody know, everybody does have dates there, is a meeting place.'

Many nights he went there before he get to know how to move around the city, and see them fellars and girls waiting, looking at they wristwatch, watching the people coming up the escalator from the tube. You could tell that they waiting for somebody, the way how they getting on. Leaning up there, reading the *Evening News*, or smoking a cigarette, or walking round the circle looking at clothes in the glasscase, and every time people come up the escalator, they watching to see, and if the person not there, they relaxing to wait till the next tube come. All these people there, standing up waiting for somebody. And then you would see a sharp piece of skin come up the escalator, in a sharp coat, and she give the ticket collector she ticket and look around, and same time the fellar who waiting throw away his cigarette and you could see a happy look in his face, and the girl come and hold his arm and laugh, and he look at his wrist-watch. Then the two of them walk up the steps and gone to the Circus, gone somewhere, to the theatre, or the cinema, or just to walk around and watch the big life in the Circus.

Lord, that is life for you, that is it. To meet a craft there, and take she out some place.

'What you think, Moses?' he ask Moses.

'Ah, in you I see myself, how I was when I was new to London. All them places is like nothing to me now. Is like when you back home and you hear fellars talk about Times Square and Fifth Avenue, and Charing Cross and gay Paree. You say to yourself, "Lord, them places must be sharp." Then you get a chance and you see them for yourself, and is like nothing.'

'You remember that picture *Waterloo Bridge*, with Robert Taylor? I went down by the bridge the other night, and stand up and watch the river.'

'Take it easy,' Moses say wearily.

But Galahad feel like a king living in London. The first time he take a craft out, he dress up good, for one of the first things he do after he get a work was to stock up with clothes like stupidness, as if to make up for all the hard times when he didn't have nice things to wear.

So this is Galahad dressing up for the date: he clean his shoes until they shine, then he put on a little more Cherry Blossom and give then a extra shine, until he could see his face in the leather. Next he put on a new pair of socks—nylon splice in the heel and the toe. He have to put on woollen underwear, though is summer. Then the shirt—a white Van Heusen. Which tie to wear? Galahad have so much tie that whenever he open the cupboard is only tie he seeing in front of him, and many times he just put out his hand and make a grab, and whichever one come he wear. But for this date he choose one of those woollen ties that the bottom cut off. Before he put on trousers and jacket he comb his hair. That is a big operation for Galahad, because he grow the hair real long and bushy, and it like a clump of grass on the head. First, he wet the hair with some water, then he push his finger in the haircream jar and scoop out some. He rub the cream on his hands, then he rub his hands in his head. The only mirror in the room is a small one that Galahad have tie on to the electric light cord, and the way he have it, it just a little bit higher than he is, so while he combing the grass he have to sort of look up and not forward. So this comb start going through the grass, stumbling across some big knot in Galahad hair, and water flying from the head as the comb make a pass, and Galahad concentrating on the physiognomy, his forehead wrinkled and he turning the head this way and that. Then afterwards he taking the brush and touching the hair like a tonsorial specialist, here and there, and when he finish, the hair comb well.

When Galahad put on trousers the seam could cut you, and the jacket fitting square on the shoulders. One thing with Galahad since he hit London, no foolishness about clothes: even Moses surprise at the change. Now if you bounce up Galahad one morning by the tube station when he coming from work, you won't believe is the same fellar you did see coasting in the park the evening before. He have on a old cap that was brown one time, but black now with grease and fingerprint, and a jacket that can't see worse days, and a corduroy trousers that would shame them ragandbone man. The shoes have big hole, like they laughing, and so Galahad fly out the tube station, his eyes red and bleary, and his body tired and bent up like a piece of wire, and he only stop to get a *Daily Express* by the station. For Galahad, like Moses, pick up a night work, because it have more money in it. He wasn't doing electrician, but with overtime he grossing about ten so why worry? So while other people going to work, Galahad coming from work. He does cross the road and go by the bakery and buy a hot bread to take home and eat. This time so, as he walking, he only studying sleep, and if a friend bawl out 'Aye, Galahad!' he pass him straight because his mind groggy and tired.

But when you dressing, you dressing. Galahad tailor is a fellar in the Charing Cross Road that Moses put him on to and the tailor surprise that Galahad know all the smartest and latest cut. He couldn't palm off no slack work on the old Galahad at all. And one thing, Galahad not stinting on money for clothes, because he get enough tone when he land up in tropical and watchekong. Don't matter if the test tell him twenty guineas or thirtyfive pounds, Galahad know what he want, and he tell the fellar is all right, you go ahead, cut that jacket so and so, and don't forget I want a twenty-three bottom on the trousers.

And the crowning touch is a long silver chain hanging from the fob, and coming back into the side pocket.

So, cool as a lord, the old Galahad walking out to the road, with plastic raincoat hanging on the arm, and the eyes not missing one sharp craft that pass, bowing his head in a polite 'Good evening' and not giving a blast if they answer or not. This is London, this is life oh lord, to walk like a king with money in your pocket, not a worry in the world.

Is one of those summer evenings, when it look like night would never come, a magnificent evening, a powerful evening, rent finish paying, rations in the cupboard, twenty pounds in the bank, and a nice piece of skin waiting under the big clock in Piccadilly Tube Station. The sky blue, sun shining, the girls ain't have on no coats to hide the legs.

'Mummy, look at that black man!' A little child, holding on to the mother hand, look up at Sir Galahad.

'You mustn't say that, dear!' The mother chide the child.

But Galahad skin like rubber at this stage, he bend down and pat the child cheek, and the child cower and shrink and begin to cry.

'What a sweet child!' Galahad say, putting on the old English accent, 'What's your name?'

But the child mother uneasy as they stand up there on the pavement with so many white people around: if they was alone she might have talked a little, and ask Galahad what part of the world he come from, but instead she pull the child along and she look at Galahad and give a sickly sort of smile, and the old Galahad, knowing how it is, smile back and walk on.

If that episode did happen around the first time when he land up in London, oh Lord! he would have run to the boys, telling them he have big ballad. But at this stage Galahad like duck back when rain fall—everything running off. Though it used to have times when he lay down there on the bed in the basement room in the Water, and all the experiences like that come to him, and he say 'Lord, what it is we people do in this world that we have to suffer so? What it is we want that the white people and them find it so hard to give? A little work, a little food, a little place to sleep. We not asking for the sun, or the moon. We only want to get by, we don't even want to get on.' And Galahad would take his hand from under the blanket, as he lay there studying how the night before he was in the lavatory and two white fellars come in and say how these black bastards have the lavatory dirty, and they didn't know that he was there, and when he come out they say hello mate have a cigarette. And Galahad watch the colour of his hand, and talk to it, saying, 'Colour, is you that causing all this, you know. Why the hell you can't be blue, or red or green, if you can't be white? You know is you that cause a lot of misery in the world. Is not me, you know, is you! I ain't do anything to infuriate the people and them, is you! Look at you, you so black and innocent, and this time so you causing misery all over the world!'

So Galahad talking to the colour Black, as if is a person, telling it that is not *he* who causing botheration in the place, but Black, who is a worthless thing for making trouble all about. 'Black, you see what you cause to happen yesterday? I went to look at that room that Ram tell me about in the Gate, and as soon as the landlady see you she say the room let already. She ain't even give me a chance to say good morning. Why the hell you can't change colour?'

Galahad get so interested in this theory about Black that he went to tell Moses. 'Is not we that the people don't like,' he tell Moses, 'is the colour Black.' But the day he went to Moses with this theory Moses was in a evil mood, because a new friend did just get in a thing with some white fellars by Praed Street, near Paddington Station. The friend was standing up there reading in the window about rooms to let and things to sell, and it had a notice saying Keep the Water White, and right there the friend start to get on ignorant (poor fellar, he was new in London) and want to get in big argument with the white people standing around.

So Moses tell Galahad, 'Take it easy, that is a sharp theory, why you don't write about it.'

Anyway all thought like that out of Galahad mind as he out on this summer evening, walking down the Bayswater Road on his way to the Circus. He go into the gardens, and begin to walk down to the Arch, seeing so much cat about the place, laying down on the grass, sitting and talking, all of them in pretty summer colours, the grass green, the sky blue, sun shining, flowers growing, the fountains spouting water, and Galahad Esquire strolling through all of this, three-four pounds in the pocket, sharp clothes on—lord oh lord—going to meet a first-class craft that waiting for him in the Circus. Once or twice, as he get a smile here and there, he mad to forget Daisy and try to make some headway in the park.

By the Arch, he meet one of the boys.

'Where you going,' the test say.

'Have a date, man, going to pick up a little thing down the road.'

'Listen, listen here to the rarse this man talking, about how colonials shouldn't come to Brit'n, that the place overflowing with spades.'

'I ain't have time, man, I late already.'

'Lend me ten shillings.'

'I can't make it now, come round tomorrow.'

'Oh God ease me up, man. A cup of char?'

Galahad give him a shilling and move away from the Arch, watching up at the clock on the Odeon although he have wristwatch. The clock saying halfpast seven and he have to meet Daisy at eight. He start to walk a little faster, but was five past when he find himself in the Circus.

Always, from the first time he went there to see Eros and the lights, that circus have a magnet for him, that circus represent life, that circus is the beginning and the ending of the world. Every time he go there, he have the same feeling like when he see it the first night, drink coca-cola, any time is guinness time, bovril and the fireworks, a million flashing lights, gay laughter, the wide doors of theatres, the huge posters, everready batteries, rich people going into tall hotels, people going to the theatre, people sitting and standing and walking and talking and laughing and buses and cars and Galahad Esquire, in all this, standing there in the big city, in London. Oh Lord.

He went down the steps into the station, and Daisy was expecting him to come by tube so she watching the escalators, and he walk up behind her and he put his hands over she eyes, and that evening people in the tube station must be bawl to see black man so familiar with white girl. But Galahad feeling too good to bother about the loud tones in them people eyes. Tonight is his night. This was something he uses to dream about in Trinidad. The time when he was leaving, Frank tell him: 'Boy, it have bags of white pussy in London, and you will eat till you tired.' And now, the first date, in the heart of London, dressed to kill, ready to escort the number around the town, anywhere she want to go, any place at all.

Daisy was dress up plenty, she look different than when she

in the plant with a pair of jeans and a overalls on. All the grease
and dirt wash off the hands, the hair comb well, the dress is a
sort of cotton but it have all sorts of coloured designs on it
and it look pretty, and she have on lipstick for so. She look real
sharp, and when he was coming up he notice the trim legs, and
the straight lines of the nylons, and the highheel shoes.

Daisy move his hands and say, 'Oh, it's you. I thought you
were coming by tube.' And she look a little embarrass, but
Galahad didn't notice.

'What time it is now in Trinidad?' Galahad look at the big
clock, watching for Trinidad; the island so damn small it only
have a dot and the name. 'That is where I come from,' he tell
Daisy, 'you see how far it is from England?'

'We'll be late,' Daisy say.

'Which part you want to go,' Galahad ask, 'anywhere at all.
Tonight we on a big splurge.'

'They're showing *The Gladiator* at the Hippodrome, and I
want to see it.'

'Pictures! Is pictures you want to go to tonight?'

'Well it's Sunday and all the theatres are closed.'

'Who acting in *The Gladiator*?'

'Victor Mature.'

'Well if that is what you want, all right. But I was thinking
we could go some place and have a good time, being as is the
only night I have off for the whole week, and you too.'

So they went to this theatre that showing *The Gladiator*, and
Galahad feeling good with this piece of skin walking with him.
But when he look at prices to enter, he couldn't help saying how
it was a lot of money, not that he mind, but he know that that
same picture would come down in the Water and show for two
and six.

'This is the West End,' Daisy remind him.

'All right, even if is a pound we still going.'

After the picture they went to a restaurant and eat a big

meal, and Galahad buy a bottle of French wine, telling the
waiter to bring the best.

The summer night descend with stars, they walking hand in
hand, and Galahad feeling hearts.

'It was a lovely evening—' Daisy began.

'Come and go in the yard,' Galahad say.

'What?' Daisy say.

'The yard. Where I living.'

All this time he was stalling, because he feeling sort of shame
to bring the girl in that old basement room, but if the date end
in fiasco he know the boys would never finish giving him tone
for spending all that money and not eating.

Daisy start to hesitate but he make haste and catch a number
twelve, telling she that it all on the way home. When they hop
off by the Water she was still getting on prim, but Galahad
know was only grandcharge, and besides the old blood getting
hot, so he walk Daisy brisk down the road, and she quiet as a
mouse. They went down the basement steps and Galahad
fumble for the key, and when he open the door a whiff of stale
food and old clothes and dampness and dirt come out the door
and he only waiting to hear what Daisy would say.

But she ain't saying nothing, and he walk through the passage
and open the door and put the light on.

Daisy sit down on the bed and Galahad say: 'You want a
cup of char?' And without waiting for any answer he full the
pot in the tap and put it on the ring and turn the gas on. He
feel so excited that he had to light a cigarette, and he keep
saying Take it easy to himself.

'Is this your room?' Daisy say, looking around and shifting
about as if she restless.

'Yes,' Galahad say. 'You like it?'

'Yes,' Daisy say.

Galahad throw a copy of *Ebony* to her and she begin to turn
the pages.

With all the excitement Galahad taking off the good clothes

carefully and slowly, putting the jacket and trousers on the hanger right away, and folding up the shirt and putting it in the drawer.

When the water was boiling he went to the cupboard and take out a packet of tea, and he shake some down in the pot.

Daisy look at him as if he mad.

'Is that how you make tea?' she ask.

'Yes,' Galahad say. 'No foolishness about it. Tea is tea—you just drop some in the kettle. If you want it strong, you drop plenty. If you want it weak, you drop little bit. And so you make a lovely cuppa.'

He take the kettle off and rest it on a sheet of *Daily Express* on the ground. He bring two cups, a spoon, a bottle of milk and a packet of sugar.

'Fix up,' he say, handing Daisy a cup.

They sit down there sipping the tea and talking.

'You get that raise the foreman was promising you?' Galahad ask, for something to say.

'What did you say? You know it will take me some time to understand everything you say. The way you West Indians speak!'

'What wrong with it?' Galahad ask. 'Is English we speaking.'

And so he coasting a little oldtalk until the tea finish, and afterwards he start to make one set of love to Daisy.

'It was battle royal in that basement, man,' he tell Moses afterwards, and he went on to give a lot of detail, though all of that is nothing to a old veteran like Moses, is only to Galahad is new because is the first time with a white number. Moses smile a knowing smile, a tired smile, and 'Take it easy,' he tell Sir Galahad.

*　　*　　*

Big City come from an orphanage in one of the country district in Trinidad. When he was a little fellar, he hear some people talking about the music the norphanage band does play. But instead of hearing 'music' Big City thought he hear 'fusic' and since that time nobody could ever get him to say music.

'Listen to that sharp piece of fusic by Mantovanee, Moses.'

'Man Big City, the word is "music" not "fusic".'

'Ah, you only trying to tie me up. You think I don't know English?'

When Big City get big he left the norphanage and he went in the army in Trinidad. He used to eat so much food, you couldn't see him behind the plate. It was there that he get the name Big City. He always talking about the big cities of the world.

'Big city for me,' he would say. 'None of this smalltime village life for me. Is New York and London and Paris, that is big life. You think I going to stay in Trinidad when the war over? This small place? No, not this old man.'

Big City had a way, he used to be grumpy and vex with everybody until it was payday. You couldn't tell him a word until Friday come.

'Big City, what happening man?'

'Listen, why you —ing me up so? Why you don't — off and leave me alone?'

'But I only ask you what's happening, man.'

'Leave me alone, get to — out.'

All the week he like that, but when he get pay on Friday, he sitting down on the counter—he used to be in the stores—and picking his toes and smiling, and calling out to everybody who come in.

'Come and have a drink,' he would invite friend and stranger. 'I have a bottle here.' He never mop a drink from anybody, it was he who always giving, and he would talk about all the big places in the world, how after the war he was going to work on ships and go all about.

Little later that same day, some fellars would say: 'Big City, how about some wapee?'

'Listen to this man! I don't gamble, boy.'

But half an hour after Big City kneeling down in the circle, a dollar bill crumple up and stick in his earhole, and some small change before him.

By the time Monday come around he revert to 'haul your arse' and 'stop —ing me up' when anybody talk to him.

War over, and Big City begin to work on ship and travel all about. One day the ship dock in London and he went to Piccadilly Circus and watch the big life. When the ship sail Big City stay behind.

But with all the travelling and experience he still remain convinced that it ain't have no word like 'music'.

'Where you going, Big City?'

'Nottingham Gate.'

'Is not Nottingham, boy, is Notting Hill.'

'You trying to — me up?'

'All right, all right. Where you living now?'

'Shepherd's Hill.'

How it is that Big City get a car, nobody know. But all of a sudden the boys see him driving car all over London.

'Where you get that car, Big City?'

'Mind your own —ing business. You want a drive?'

The week he get this car he meet with a accident with a number fortynine bus and he had was to go to court. He went around by Moses moaning, with a lot of forms he had to full up. Big City always confuse when he have forms to full up, and in the old Brit'n it have bags of that to do. He and the English woman he living with always arguing, is not that way, no, you put the date in the wrong place, man, why you so stupid, you can't see where it say date of birth in the next line?

So to avoid contention with the wife he does always go round by Moses whenever he have forms to full up.

'How this accident happen?' Moses ask.

'Boy, them —ing bus drivers can't drive, I was going slow down by Gloucestershire Road—'

'You mean Gloucester Road.'

'Stop —ing me up, man, I tell you Gloucestershire Road. And same time this bus fly round the corner—'

Moses help Big City to full up the forms.

Another thing, he like to go in for football pool, but up to now he don't know how to full up the forms properly, and every week he round by Moses.

'Boy, the day I win that £75,000, oh lord! It would be hell in London city, boy. You know I nearly had them last week? I was only one draw out—you sure you marking the nought in the right place?'

'Man Big City,' Moses say, 'is time you learn to full up the coupon for yourself, you know. It not hard. Let me show you.'

But Big City went on as if Moses didn't speak. 'Blackpool playing Aston Villa this week,' he say, 'that is a sure draw. What you think of Arsenal?'

'Listen,' Moses say. 'I tired telling you, I don't believe that football pool is for me. If I ever get money is by the sweat of the brow, and not through winning anything.'

'You making joke, Moses! Last week two fellars win £75,000. Why you don't take a chance? Is only a tanner a week I does invest. Why you don't join the Littlewoods Happy Circle of Investigators? Look it have a place there where you can put your name and address on the coupon, and they will start sending you forms.'

'Big City,' Moses say again, tired out with helping full the form week after week, 'make a effort to learn, boy. You see where it mark eight selections? You have to make a nought in eight places. You can't go wrong even if you try. Right in the spaces here.'

But Big City enter the pools every week and never full up a form himself yet. He try Littlewoods for two months, then he give it up and switch to Shermans. After that he went to Hills, then Vernon, then Cope, then he went back to Littlewoods.

'Never mind boy,' he tell Moses, 'one day I will win that £75,000 and then you know what?'

'No, what?'

'Big city, boy, big city. Paris, Brussels, Berlin, Rome, Bagdan, then after the States, San Francis, Chicago, New York, then after one of them yacht to sail in the Mediteran. And women? Women for so! Where all those bigshots does go? On the River, in Italy.'

'And what about the car you have now, you will give it to your good friend Moses who full up the form for you, or when you have all that money you forget your friends?'

'No boy. You know what I will do? I would like to have money, and buy out a whole street of house, and give it to the boys and say: "Here, look place to live." And I would put a notice on all the boards: "Keep the Water Coloured, No Rooms For Whites." '

'But Big City, you only have mouth, man. I sure if you win all that money you head straight back for Trinidad to eat a breadfruit and saltfish and go Maracas Bay to bathe in the sea.'

'Who, me? No boy. I not saying I mightn't go back. Come to think of it is a good idea to go back like a lord and let all them bitches see how much money I have. But wherever I roam, I will land back in the old Brit'n. Nine-ten years I live here now, and I get to like the place. But Moses, serious boy, if you get that £75,000 in the pools what you would do?'

'I never think about that, I tell you. I would never get money that way.'

'You never know your luck, old man. Look, you remember in '51 it had a Jamaica fellar what win some money in the pools. You know what he do? He send for the whole family and he buy three-four house in London. Now, he living easy, and that wasn't even a £75,000. You could sit on your tail and say you won't get it, but tell me Moses, *if* you get it, what you will do?'

'I don't know, I tell you. I does always think poor, the old brain can't imagine what to do with all that money.'

But after City leave him Moses used to think bout that money, how it would solve all the problems in the world. He used to see all his years in London pile up one on top of the other, and he getting no place in a hurry, and the years going by, and the thought make him frighten sometimes.

Although Big City have no work, yet he always have money, for he does go in for big deals, though nobody ever know what them big deals is. Once he went away for three months and when he come back, he tell the boys he went for holiday in Wales. But everybody suspect that the law catch up with City.

It have no other lime in London that Big City like more than to coast by Marble Arch at the Orator's Corner on a summer evening and listen to them fellars talking about how the government this and that, or making big discussion on the colour problem. In fact, this lime is a regular for the boys. On any Sunday in the summer, in the sweet, lazy summer when them days like they would never done, when all the fog and snow gone, and night stay long to come, when you could put on a hot jitterbug shirt and wear a light sharkskin pants, when them white girls have on summer frocks and you could see legs and shapes that used to hide under winter coats, when the sun shining and the sky blue and a warm wind blowing across the park, on any such Sunday evening, all the boys dressing up and coasting lime by the Arch, listening to all them reprobates and soapbox politicians, looking around to see if they could pick up something in the crowd. From east and west, north and south, the boys congregate by the Arch.

The first time Galahad ever went there, he amaze at how them fellars saying all kind of thing against the government and the country, and the police not doing them anything.

'Why is that, City?' he ask City.

'Is so it is in Brit'n,' Big City say. 'Listen, you always grumbling and cursing about something or other, why you don't go and talk to the crowd?'

'Yes, why you don't go, Galahad?' Moses start to poke fire.

'The people like to listen to the boys. I know you have a lot on the chest, this is the place to get it off.'

Galahad start to hem. 'I can't just go and talk like that,' he say.

'I know the fellar who talking on the colour problem,' City say, 'I will tell him that you can give the people the real dope on the question. What you say?'

Galahad start to grin foolishly and shrug his shoulders and shift his foot but Moses, egging him on for so, until at last it look like to save face he really have to say something.

Big City went and talk to the fellar on the platform, and the fellar raise his hands and tell the crowd: 'Ladies and gentlemen, I myself am not a Colonial, but one who has been listening has kindly volunteered to come forward and tell you more about the question than I can.'

The boys cheer Galahad, and Galahad, feeling like a fool, had was to go up on the platform, because he couldn't back out at this stage. But one set of fright take him, he don't know what to say.

'Ladies and gentlemen—' he began.

'Talk louder man,' Big City say. 'We can't hear you.'

'The truth about this whole question,' Galahad went on desperately, 'is that we want work to do. I here in this country a long time and I can't get a regular work—'

'The people can't understand you boy,' Big City was out to make it hard for Galahad. 'Talk good English.'

'Give me a chance, Big City,' Galahad say, finding it easier to address one man in the crowd, and everybody start to laugh.

'Tell them about the time the foreman call you a nigger,' Big City say.

'Give me a chance, Big City,' Galahad say.

But Big City start to exchange words with Galahad, and all the people looking at the two of them and laughing, and Galahad getting more and more vex, until at last he fly down from the platform as if he going to attack Big City. But the boys hold him back, though in truth Big City is a big fellar and Galahad wouldn't have stand a chance.

All the same, Galahad had it in for Big City from that time, and he went about telling everybody that the next time he meet him he would beat him like a snake. Nobody pay Galahad any mind, but one evening, right there by the Arch under some trees, he was with the boys liming when they see Big City coming down the road.

'Ah,' Moses say, stoking the fire, 'look Big City coming, Galahad. Now is the time to beat him.'

Now Galahad is a fellar who full of grandcharge. One time in Trinidad he had an enemy he was always threatening to beat. Galahad had a brother and he used to tell him: 'Listen, whenever Roy passing by here, I will charge him as if I going to beat him flat, but whenever you see me do that, you must run and come and hold me back.' The brother agree, and so Galahad used to rush up to Roy whenever he passing by the house, and make as if he going to attack, and the brother would come and hold him back. This happen three-four times, until one day when Galahad charge, the brother wasn't there. Roy hold on to Galahad and give him a good licking.

Now, when he look and see Big City coming down the road in truth, he get frighten and keep quiet, though Moses urging him on.

Big City come up and say: 'I hear you looking for me, Galahad.'

Galahad grin foolishly and say: 'What happening, Big City?'

Big City know he could of beat Galahad, so he didn't bother with him. He just stand up and talk a little while with the boys, then he take off after a thing that was walking by.

As soon as he get a safe distance away Galahad kneel down and make the sign of the cross and say: 'I will beat Big City like a snake the next time we meet.'

Big City used to have dreams, and he believe those dreams as if they happen in truth.

'Last night,' he tell Moses, 'I went to see Lady —. You never see a house like that, boy. Four inch carpet in the hallway, butler opening the door, whisky and soda on the table, and a high tea spread out on the sideboard. I spend the night there. I meet Lord —, and other important people.'

'Ah Big City, you had another dream.'

'If I lie I die, the house is near Kensington Mansion, where all those millionaires and diplomats does live.'

'You mean Kensington Palace.'

'Don't begin to — me up again. You think I don't know London? I been here ten years now, and it ain't have a part that I don't know. When them English people tell strangers they don't know where so and so is, I always know. From Pentonvilla right up to Musket Hill, all about by Claphand Common. I bet you can't call a name in London that I don't know where it is.'

'All right Big City, take it easy. How you meet this Lady?'

'I was coasting a lime by the Circus, and a big limousine pull up, and the driver ask me if I from the West Indies, and I say yes, and then he say that Lady — want to meet a West Indian, if I would come. So you should know I hop in the car—car, father, boy—and we drive to Millionaires Road.'

Another time he would come and say how he went to a party that had all them bigshots like what you read about in the *Evening Standard* column London Last Night.

'How your name wasn't in the papers then?'

'Oh, they wouldn't put my name. But if you look in today's *Standard* you will see the party I was telling you about. It was in the Savoy. Churchill was there ...'

*　　*　　*

Oh what a time it is when summer come to the city and all them girls throw away heavy winter coat and wearing light summer frocks so you could see the legs and shapes that was hiding away from the cold blasts and you could coast a lime in the park and negotiate ten shillings or a pound with the sports as the case may be or else they have a particular bench near

the Hyde Park Corner that they call the Play Around Section
where you could go and sit with one of them what a time
summer is because you bound to meet the boys coasting lime in
the park and you could go walking through the gardens and see
all them pretty pieces of skin taking suntan and how the old
geezers like the sun they would sit on the benches and smile
everywhere you turn the English people smiling isn't it a lovely
day as if the sun burn away all the tightness and strain that was
in their faces for the winter and on a nice day every manjack
and his brother going to the park with his girl and laying down
on the green grass and making love in the winter you would
never think that the grass would ever come green again but if
you don't keep your eyes open it look like one day the trees
naked and the next day they have clothes on sometimes walking
up to the Bayswater Road from Queensway you could look on a
winter day and see how grim the trees looking and a sort of fog
in the distance though right near to you you ain't have no fog
but that is only deceiving because if somebody down the other
side look up by where you are it would look to them as if it
have fog by where you are and this time so the sun in the sky
like a forceripe orange and it giving no heat at all and the
atmosphere like a sullen twilight hanging over the big city but it
different too bad when is summer for then the sun shine for
true and the sky blue and a warm wind blowing it look like
when is winter a kind of grey nasty colour does come to the
sky and it stay there and you forget what it like to see blue
skies like back home where blue sky so common people don't
even look up in the air and you feeling miserable and cold but
when summer come is fire in the town big times fete like
stupidness and you have to keep the blood cool for after all them
cold and wet months you like you roaring to go though to tell
truth winter don't make much difference to some of the boys
they blazing left and right as usual all the year round to talk
of all the episodes that Moses had with woman in London would
take bags of ballad Moses move through all the nationalities in

the world and then he start the circle again everybody know
how after the war them rich English family sending to the
continent to get domestic and over there all them girls think like
the newspapers say about the Jamaicans that the streets of
London paved with gold so they coming by the boatload and
the boys making contact and having big times with the girls
working during the day and coming round by the yard in the
evening for a cuppa and to hit one or two but anyone of Moses
encounter is big episode because coasting about the Water it
ain't have no man with a sharper eye than he not even Cap could
ask him for anything and one summer evening he was walking
when he spot a number and he smile and she smile back and
after a little preliminary about the weather Moses take her for
a drink in the pub and after that he coast a walk with she in
Kensington Gardens and they sit down on the grass and talk
about how lovely the city is in the summer and Moses say how
about coming to my yard she went but afterwards Moses nearly
dead with fright because the woman start to moan and gasp
and wriggle and twist up she body like a piece of wire when
Moses ask she what happen she only moaning Moses start to get
cold sweat because he know that if anything happen to the
woman and the police find her in his yard that he wouldn't
stand a chance the way how things against the boys from in
front so he begin to rub the woman down and pat she and try
to make she drink some water what happen to you Moses ask
frighten like hell that the woman might conk off on his hands
the woman only gasping and calling out for her mother and
Moses sweating just then the bell ring and Moses went to the
door and see Daniel Daniel he say boy a hell of a thing happening here man I just pick up a woman up the road and bring
she in the yard and it look like if she dying what Daniel say as
if he don't understand wait here Moses say and he run back in
the room listen he tell the woman my friend come and you have
to go put on your clothes by the time Moses went and call
Daniel inside the woman was calm and cool as if nothing happen

she look all right to me Daniel say eyeing the piece as if he ready to charge but Moses was too frighten to keep the woman around though she sit down on the bed and begin to talk calmly boy he tell Daniel you wouldn't believe me but the woman did look as if she going to dead you only lying because I happen to come round while you have she here Daniel say but Moses so relieve that she looking all right that he didn't bother with Daniel he just tell her to come and go right away so he take her out to the Bayswater Road to catch a bus the heel of my shoe is coming off she say will you come with me to get it fixed sure Moses say but as soon as they hop on the bus and it begin to drive off Moses hop off again and leave she going to Marble Arch what a gambol does go on in the park on them summer nights oh sometimes the girls wishing it would get dark quickly and you have them parading all down the Bayswater Road from the Arch to the Gate and you could see them fellars going up and talking for a minute and if they agree they go in the park or somewhere else together and if not the fellar walk on but these fellars that cruising they could size up the situation in one glance as they pass by and know if they like this one or that one you does meet all sorts of fellars from all walks of life don't ever be surprised at who you meet up cruising and reclining in the park it might be your boss or it might be some big professional fellar because it ain't have no discrimination when it come to that in the park in the summer see them girls in little groups here and there talking and how they could curse you never hear curse until one of them sports curse you if you approach one and she don't like your terms she tell you to — off right away and if you linger she tell you to double — off but business is brisk in the park in the summer one night one of them hustle from behind a tree pulling up her clothes and she bawl out Mary the police and if you see how them girls fade out and make races with the tight skirts holding the legs close together and the high heels going clopclop but that was no handicap when they take off it have some fellars who does go in the park only to cruise around and see what they could see you could always tell these tests they have on a coat with the collar turn up and they hand in they pocket and they breezing through the park hiding from tree to tree like if they playing hide and seek one night Moses was liming near the park and a car pull up that had a fellar and a old-looking woman in it the fellar start to talk friendly and invite Moses home for a cup of coffee and Moses went just to see what would happen and what happen was the fellar play as if he fall asleep and give Moses a free hand because it have fellars who does get big thrills that way but Moses didn't do anything because he know what the position like and even though the fellar offer him three pounds he smile and was polite and tell him that he sorry good night introducing Galahad to the night life Moses explain to him about short time and long time and how to tackle the girls and he take Galahad one night and let him loose in the park Galahad say I going to try and he broach a group under the trees about a hundred yards from the corner by the Arch but from the time he begin to talk the girl tell him to — off Galahad stand up to argue but Moses pull him away those girls not catholic at all Galahad say Moses say it have some of them who don't like the boys and is all the fault of Cap because Cap don't like to pay let us cut through the park and go by Hyde Park Corner Galahad say when they reach there Moses pick up a sharp thing who was talking to two English fellars and he take her to the yard afterwards the girl tell him how she used to take heroin at one time and she show him the marks on her arm where she inject the kick Moses stay with the thing regularly for a week then he get tired and tell Cap he have a girl if he interested and Cap give the usual answer so Moses tell him to come in the yard in the night that the girl would be there Cap went and Moses left the two of them in the room and went for a walk when he come back three hours later Cap was in the bathroom and the thing was standing up before the gas fire warming up the treasury your friend have any money she ask Moses yes

Moses say he have bags of money he is the son of a Nigerian
king and when he goes back home he will rule more than a
million people the girl ask Moses if he want anything take it easy
Moses say when Cap come back Moses tell him to drop the
girl up the road and the girl went with Cap thinking that he
have plenty of money when Cap get to the corner he tell her
to wait he going to change a five-pound note as he don't go
around with small change and he left the girl standing up there
and never went back meantime Moses sit down on the bed and
the bed fall down when Cap come back he say Cap you are a
hell of a man you break my bed Cap say sorry Moses say this is
the third time you break my bed Cap say it was warm and nice
in the bed Moses say what I will tell the landlord this thing
happening so often and he had was to put a box and prop up
the bed to sleep summer does really be hearts like if you start
to live again you coast a lime by the Serpentine and go for a
row on the river or you go bathing by the Lido though the
water never warm no matter how hot the sun is you would be
feeling hot out of the water but the minute you jump in you
start to shiver and have to get out quick but it does be as if
around that time of the year something strange happen to everybody they all smiling and as if they living for the first time so
you get to wondering if it ain't have a certain part of the population what does lie low during the cold months and only take to
the open when summer come for it have some faces in the Water
that Moses never see until summer come or maybe they have
enough money to go Montego Bay in winter and come back
to the old Brit'n when they know the weather would be nice
listen to this ballad what happen to Moses one summer night
one splendid summer night with the sky brilliant with stars
like in the tropics he was liming in Green Park when a English
fellar come up to him and say you are just the man I am looking
for who me Moses say yes the man say come with me Moses
went wondering what the test want and the test take him to a
blonde who was standing up under a tree and talk a little so

Moses couldn't hear but Blondie shake her head then he take
Moses to another one who was sitting on a bench and she say
yes so the test come back to Moses and want to pay Moses to
go with the woman Moses was so surprise that he say yes
quickly and he went with the thing and the test hover in the
background afterwards he ask Moses if he would come again
and Moses say yes it look like a good preposition to me I don't
mind and he carry on for a week the things that does happen in
this London people wouldn't believe when you tell them they
would cork their ears when you talk and say that isn't true but
some ballad happen in the city that people would bawl if they
hear right there in Hyde Park how them sports must bless the
government for this happy hunting ground the things that
happen there in the summer hard to believe one night two
sports catch a fellar hiding behind some bushes with a flash
camera in his hand they mash up the camera and beat the
fellar where all these women coming from you never know but
every year the ranks augmented with fresh blood from the
country districts who come to see the big life in London and the
bright lights also lately in view of the big set of West Indians
that storming Brit'n it have a lot of dark women who in the
racket too they have to make a living and you could see them
here and there with the professionals walking on the Bayswater
Road or liming in the park learning the tricks of the trade it
have some white fellars who feel is a big thrill to hit a black
number and the girls does make them pay big money but as far
as spades hitting spades it ain't have nothing like that for a
spade wouldn't hit a spade when it have so much other talent
on parade don't think that you wouldn't meet real class in the
park even in big society it have hustlers one night Moses meet
a pansy by Marble Arch tube station and from the way the test
look at him Moses know because you could always tell these
tests unless you real green you have a lovely tie the pansy say
yes Moses say you have a lovely hat yes Moses say you have a
very nice coat yes Moses say everything I have is nice I like you

the pansy say I like you too Moses say and all this time he
want to dead with laugh I have a lovely model staying in my flat
in Knightsbridge the pansy say she likes to go with men but I
don't like that sort of thing myself would you like to come to
my flat sure Moses say we will go tomorrow night as I have an
important engagement tonight I will meet you right here by
the station the test say but so many people are here Moses say I
might miss you if you don't see me you can phone but what
will we do when I come to your flat Moses say playing stupid
and the test tell him what and what they wouldn't do one night
he and Galahad was walking up Inverness Terrace when a car
pass going slow and the door open and a fellar fling one of the
sports out the poor girl fall down and roll to the pavement all
the other sports in the area rally and run up to she and pick
she up and ask she what happen she say she went with the
fellar but he didn't want to pay and she give him two cuff in
his face and he pitch she out the car another night a big
Jamaican fellar take two home and had them running out of the
house and he throw their clothes for them from the window
people wouldn't believe you when you tell them the things that
happen in the city but the cruder you are the more the girls
like you you can't put on any English accent for them or play
ladeda or tell them you studying medicine in Oxford or try to
be polite and civilise they don't want that sort of thing at all
they want you to live up to the films and stories they hear about
black people living primitive in the jungles of the world that is
why you will see so many of them African fellars in the city
with their hair high up on the head like they ain't had a trim
for years and with scar on their face and a ferocious expression
going about with some real sharp chicks the cruder you are
the more they like you the whole blasted set of them frustrated
like if they don't know what it is all about what happen to you
people Moses ask a cat one night and she tell him how the black
boys so nice and could give them plenty thrills people wouldn't
believe or else they would cork their ears and say they don't

want to know but the higher the society the higher the kicks they want one night Moses meet a nice woman driving in a car in Piccadilly and she pick him up and take him to a club in Knightsbridge where it had a party bags of women and fellars all about drinking champagne and whisky this girl who pick him up get high and start to dance the cancan with some other girls when they fling their legs up in the air they going around to the tables where the fellars sitting Moses sit down there wondering how this sort of thing happening in a place where only the high and the mighty is but with all of that they feel they can't get big thrills unless they have a black man in the company and when Moses leave afterwards they push five pounds in his hand and pat him on the back and say that was a jolly good show it have a lot of people in London who cork their ears and wouldn't listen but if they get the chance they do the same thing themselves everybody look like they frustrated in the big city the sex life gone wild you would meet women who beg you to go with them one night a Jamaican with a woman in Chelsea in a smart flat with all sorts of surrealistic painting on the walls and contemporary furniture in the G-plan the poor fellar bewildered and asking questions to improve himself because the set-up look like the World of Art but the number not interested in passing on any knowledge she only interested in one thing and in the heat of emotion she call the Jamaican a black bastard though she didn't mean it as an insult but as a compliment under the circumstances but the Jamaican fellar get vex and he stop and say why the hell you call me a black bastard and he thump the woman and went away all these things happen in the blazing summer under the trees in the park on the grass with the daffodils and tulips in full bloom and a sky of blue oh it does really be beautiful then to hear the birds whistling and see the green leaves come back on the trees and in the night the world turn upside down and everybody hustling that is life that is London oh lord Galahad say when the sweetness of summer get in him he say he would never leave the old Brit'n as long as he live and Moses sigh a long sigh like a man who live life and see nothing at all in it and who frighten as the years go by wondering what it is all about.

*   *   *

It had a fellar call Five Past Twelve. A test look at him and say, 'Boy, you black like midnight.' Then the test take a second look and say, 'No, you more like Five Past Twelve.'

Five come from Barbados. During the war when Yankee was opening up base in Trinidad fellars was making a lot of money and the Five went to take part. One time he was taking out a Trinidad girl and the boys in the district didn't like it. They tell Five to leave the girl alone but Five ain't pay them no mind: the next night he was coasting with the girl round Queen's Park Savannah. The boys get a tin of pitch oil and throw on Five and start to run after him with a box of matches.

Right after the war Five come to England to hustle and the next thing you know he had on RAF uniform doing three years with them. When the three years up Five get a work driving truck across the country.

Five was a fellar, from the time he see you, he out to borrow money. You hardly have time to ask him what happening than he ask you if you could lend him ten shillings till Friday please God. So that all the boys start to take in front: from the time they see Five, they ask him to lend them two and six, that things really brown.

'Ah,' Five say, disappointed, 'you only asking me because you know I was going to ask you.'

'No Five, I really bawling. Lend me two and six.'

Five have woman all over London, and no sooner he hit the big city than he fly round by Moses to find out what happening, which part have fete and so on. For Five like a fete too bad. The time when the Lord Mayor did driving through London, it had a steel band beating pan all in the Circus, and you should know Five was in the front, jumping up as if is a West Indian carnival.

'They should have more fete like this, in London,' Five tell Moses. 'They too slack in this city the people too quiet. I wonder when the Lord Mayor would take a drive again?'

'If you in town on Saturday,' Moses say, 'Harris giving a dance in St Pancras Hall.'

'But how you mean!' Five say. 'I must go to that, boy.'

Harris is a fellar who like to play ladeda, and he like English customs and thing, he does be polite and say thank you and he does get up in the bus and the tube to let woman sit down, which is a thing even them Englishmen don't do. And when he dress, you think is some Englishman going to work in the city, bowler and umbrella, and briefcase tuck under the arm, with *The Times* fold up in the pocket so the name would show, and he walking upright like if is he alone who alive in the world. Only thing, Harris face black.

One time Moses meet Harris by Queensway buying daffodil from a barrow boy.

'Ah, you going in for horticulture now,' Moses tone.

The old Harris smile. 'No, I'm going to have high tea with Lord —'s daughter, and I thought it would be a nice gesture to take some flowers along.'

Man, when Harris start to spout English for you, you realise that you don't really know the language. Harris moving among the bigshots, because of the work he does do, which is to organise little fetes here and there, like dance and party and so on. And every time Harris worried if Five would turn up, because Five like to make rab and have Harris feeling small, though it does only be fun he making, for he not a malicious fellar at heart.

That fete in St Pancras Hall the Saturday night was big times. Harris had everything under control. He had a steel band to play music, a bar for the boys to drink, and he know already that bags of people coming to the fete from the number of tickets that he sell. So there Harris is, standing up by the door in black suit and bow tie, greeting all English people with a pleasant good evening and how do you do, and a not so pleasant greeting for the boys, for if is one thing he fraid is that the boys make rab and turn the dance into a brawl. That never happen in a big way yet, but still he always have the fear, and he always have a word for the boys as they come: 'See and behave yourselves like proper gentlemen, there are a lot of English people here tonight so don't make a disgrace of yourselves.'

Of course, none of the boys paying to go to Harris dance, they only breezing in and saying good evening Mr Harris. Harris can't do anything about that, and in order to avoid contention by the door he does only shrug his shoulders and allow them to pass. But all the time he keeping an eye open for Five, praying that he would be out of town on business, for Five does make it his business to pick on Harris because he so ladeda.

But Five never fail to appear, with four or five white chicks holding on to him. And from the minute he burst through the door with a long jacket draping across the knees he bawling out: 'Harris, you old reprobate! What happening?'

Harris naturally feel bad that in front of all the English people Five getting on so. He pull Five to one side while the girls go inside.

'Listen man,' Harris plead with Five, 'I want you to make an effort to behave and comport yourself properly tonight. I have a distinguished gentleman and his wife here tonight. Try to get on decently just for once.'

But nothing could rouse Five more than to approach him like this.

'But Harris man, you looking prosperous, things going good with you. I hear you did make bags of money out of that fete you had in Kilburn last Saturday. You think you will make a lot tonight? I hear you have steel band—oh God, fete like stupidness!'

'I am warning you Five,' Harris say. 'If you behave disgracefully I shall have to put you out.'

Five stand back and look at Harris. 'You know you wouldn't do that to your good friend,' he say. 'Man, sometimes you get on like if we didn't grow up together, don't mind you born in Jamaica and spent time there before you come to Trinidad. You remember them lime we used to coast by Gilda Club in Charlotte Street in Port of Spain? You remember the night when Mavis make you buy ten rum for she, and then she went behind the rumshop and tell you to come.'

Harris look around desperately. 'Don't talk so loudly, man,' he tell Five. 'It seems you are drunk already. I hope you haven't brought any weed here tonight.'

'How you mean, I must hit a weed before I get high,' Five say. 'Later on when you finish come and see me and we will go in the back and have a puff.'

'I won't touch that disgusting drug,' Harris say, 'and you had better not smoke it here. I am warning you, Five. I really have distinguished people here—'

'Ah, you does say so every time I come to any of your fete,' Five say. 'You think you could fool me? You forget I know you from back home. Is only since you hit Brit'n that you getting on so English.'

And with that Five push past Harris and float into the ballroom looking for the cats he bring with him.

By the door poor Harris wipe his face with a white handkerchief.

'Moses,' he say, when Moses appear with a frauline, 'please keep an eye on Five for me tonight. I don't want any trouble.'

Moses say, 'Sure, Harris. Let me introduce you to my girl.'

'Pleased to meet you,' Harris say quickly, for plenty people coming in.

Behind Moses Tolroy appear with a English chick, and behind him Ma and Tanty, and behind them Lewis with a little thing that he pick up to help him live bachelor life.

Tolroy and his girl go in quiet, followed by Lewis and his girl, but Tanty tug Ma and make her stand up.

'Harris!' Tanty scream out. 'You don't know me? You don't remember neighbour who used to live behind you in George Street?'

'I'm afraid—' Harris start to stammer.

'But look how big the boy get!' Tanty bawl. 'I didn't believe Tolroy when he tell me. Tolroy say how you living in London for a long time, and that you doing well for yourself. I tell Tolroy: "Not little Harris what used to run about the barrack-yard in shirttail!" And Tolroy say yes, is you self. I tell him I don't believe, so he say come tonight to the dance and you will see for yourself. Well, to tell you the truth, I don't go anywhere at all, you could ask Ma here, but when I hear that is you who giving this fete I say I must come and see you. Ma, look at little Harris how big he get! But the years pass quickly!'

'Yes, yes, I remember you,' Harris say quickly, giving Tanty a push.

But Tanty didn't budge. 'Don't push,' she say, 'have some respect for your elders. I not going to dance until you come inside. I want the first set with you. It still have some life in the old hen. But bless my eyesight!' she begin again as if she just come in. 'Look at little Harris what used to thief fowl egg under the house!' And she went inside with Ma shaking her head from side to side.

Inside the hall was a real jam session. The girls stand up in groups here and there, and the boys liming out by the bar, some of them with their girls. Like Marble Arch in the summer, any of Harris fete is a get-together of all the boys, wherever it happen to be. Big City, Galahad, Daniel, Cap, Bart, all of them leave the night work they have to hit this fete, and Moses as usual like a minor master of ceremonies with the boys, giving them all the latest lowdown and ballad as they coast a drink.

'All you see that?' Moses say. 'Look Tolroy bring the whole

family to Harris fete. Oh God, what it coming to now? It look like Saltfish Hall in London!'

Saltfish Hall was the name of a place in one of the small islands where it have a sign, Wash Your Foot And Jump In, and it have two bucket of water near the door, and all them old geezers come in from the fields and wash their foot and join the fete in the hall.

'Tolroy have a sharp thing with him,' the old Galahad observe.

'You did see him dancing with the old lady?' Big City say. Oh lord, what it is happening in this London! This fete like a real bacchanal in the Princes Building in Port of Spain! Who having a drink on me?'

'Tolroy!' Moses shout, and when Tolroy come all the boys begin to give him tone.

'What happen, you couldn't leave the old lady home?'

'You think this is Jamaica? You bringing old hen to dance?'

'Who is that woman with you, Tolroy? Give me an intro, man.'

'Bring she over here to have a drink.'

All this time the steel band blasting some hot numbers and the old Five, whenever he see Harris watching him, starting to jock waist for so, and fanning with his jacket, and jumping up like if is a real carnival slackness, only to make Harris get vex. Harris moving about the crowd saying hello to everybody and hoping they are having a good time. It really look like he have some ladeda there for it have three or four of them sitting at a table in the corner drinking, but none of them dancing, though is two man and two woman.

'Harris, who is them people who sitting down there and not dancing?' Moses ask.

'Those are my personal guests,' Harris say. 'Moses, are you keeping an eye on Five for me? I am sure he has some weed on him—look, you could see from his behaviour that he is not normal. Do you think I should have him put out?'

'Take it easy,' Moses say, 'the old Five out of this world, but he ain't misbehaving yet.'

'I must go over to my guests,' Harris say.

'Have one before you go,' Moses say, but Harris was in the crowd by this time, making his way to the table in the corner.

'How are you getting on?' Harris ask one of the young women at the table, like an attendant when you trying on a new pair of shoes.

'Fine,' she say, looking up at Harris. 'The steel band music just fascinates me. How do they manage to get such melody from the oil drums?'

'Oh, they practise a lot,' Harris say. 'Is this the first time you've heard them?'

'No, I heard a band on the BBC the other evening—I don't know if it was this one.'

Harris feel it was up to him to ask the thing to dance, seeing like they look shy to take the floor, so he ask the girl and she hem a little then she get up.

Now all this time Tanty was looking for Harris, and when he take the floor with this sharp thing she spot him dancing. Tanty get up and push away dancers as she advance to Harris.

'My boy!' she say, putting she hand on his shoulder, 'I been looking for you all over. What happening, you avoiding the old lady, eh? Too much young girl here to bother with Tanty, eh?'

Harris get so vex, but he know that if he talk rough to Tanty she might get on ignorant. Lucky for him he was dancing near the outside of the crowd, so he stop and draw aside.

'Listen,' he say to Tanty, 'can't you see I am dancing with this young lady?'

'What happen for that?' Tanty say, eyeing the white girl who look so embarrass. 'You think I can't dance too? I had a set already with Tolroy, ask him.'

'Well,' Harris say, trying hard to keep his temper, 'will you kindly wait until I am finished? We shall dance the next set.'

'You too smart, when the next set come I wouldn't find you,' Tanty say, taking a firm hold of Harris. 'Tell this girl to unlace you: you know what they playing? "Fan Me Saga Boy Fan

Me," and that is my favourite calypso. These English girls don't know how to dance calypso, man. Lady, excuse him,' and before Harris know what happening Tanty swing him on the floor, pushing up she fat self against him. The poor fellar can't do anything, in two-twos Tanty had him in the centre of the floor while she swinging she fat bottom left and right.

While the other fellars calling out to one another to watch how Tanty dancing with Harris, Five was real high, out of this world, a kind of frozen smile on his face, and a look in his eyes as if he seeing things men does only see in their dreams. But he was quick enough on the draw to see the white girl stand up there helpless while Tanty take Harris away.

'Moses,' Five say, 'look one of Harris distinguished guests stand up there by sheself.'

'Go and dance with she, Galahad,' Moses say, urging him on, but Galahad hanging back.

'I bet you I dance with she,' Five say.

'I bet you you don't,' Moses say.

Five went up to the girl before she had time to make her way back to the table. Nobody don't know to this day what Five tell the girl, if he just pick she up and start to dance or if he say may I have this dance or if he say shall we. Afterwards he tell the boys he only went up and wink at she and she was in his arms before he know what was happening. But whichever way it was, Five was closehauling this number like if the band playing a slow, sentimental fox instead of Fan Me Saga Boy Fan Me.

Half the boys saying, 'Look how Tanty have Harris!' and the other half saying, 'Look at the old Five beating close to the wind with Harris girl!'

Somehow or other Harris manage to get loose from Tanty and rush to where Moses and Galahad standing.

'Moses!' he say, 'I will really have to put Five Past Twelve out of the hall. He has been smoking weed and he is not responsible for his actions.'

'Take it easy,' Moses say, 'the old Five enjoying himself. You can't see the girl dancing with him? If she didn't want to dance she didn't have to.'

'Well, I don't like it,' Harris say. 'The next time I have a fete, attendance will be by invitation only. You boys always make a disgrace of yourselves, and make me ashamed of myself.' And Harris went off like a steam engine.

'What is the trouble here?' Big City say, coming from the Gents where he was hitting an end of weed that Five pass on to him.

'You missing big times,' Galahad say. The quarrel between them was long forgotten. 'Harris was dancing with Tanty, and now he vex that Five dancing with one of his girls.'

'Look at the old Five, man!' Moses say, admiring the dancers.

'Big City,' Galahad say, suddenly remembering the time in Hyde Park when Big City did jockey him to stand up on the platform and address the crowd, 'I bet you not as brave as Five. I bet you don't go and ask the other girl to dance—that one over there by the table sitting down with them two fellars.'

'Ah,' Big City say, 'who want to dance with them —up people? Harris always bringing some of them ladeda here.'

'I bet you don't,' Galahad say.

'You talking to Big City, boy,' Big City say.

'Ten like you don't,' Galahad say.

'I mad to go over there and ask she to dance,' City mutter.

'Harris will throw you out if you interfere with his distinguished guests,' Galahad say.

'You don't know Big City, boy,' Moses join the jockeying. 'You really don't know Big City, else you wouldn't talk so.'

By this time Big City was flying across to the table. Again, nobody ever get to find out what Big City say or what he do. Some of the boys say it was because the other girl was dancing with Five, and that give she courage. But however it was, the girl get up and start to dance with Big City

'Galahad,' Moses say, standing up in the corner and watching the proceedings, 'the things that happening here tonight never happen before. I have a feeling you will see a lot before this fete over. Watch yourself, and if you see fight run like hell, because if things open up hot I outing off fast.'

At this stage the fete in full swing, nearly everybody dancing, only the old Moses stand up in the corner with Galahad, telling him ballads about the fetes that gone before, and lowdown about some of the boys.

'I don't see Cap dancing,' Galahad observe.

'Cap take up two girl and he gone home long time,' Moses say. 'He don't stick around much if he could pick up something.'

'Bart look like if he drunk.'

'Poor fellar, he must be still studying that girl what let him down. He thought he might have found her here—when he first come in you didn't see how he went through the hall like a detective looking at everybody? Bart would never find that girl again, but he won't take my advice.'

'I see Daniel buying a lot of drinks for them girls,' Galahad say.

'That is his line, man. He like to do things like that. You will notice that the boys bring in a lot of girls, but don't buy anything for them—they just leave it to the old Daniel, and if he lucky when the fete finish he get to go home with one of them.'

Well things warm up fast in St Pancras Hall that Saturday night. Around half-past ten a Jamaican fellar bust a cocacola bottle over Five head because Five was dancing too close with his girl. Big City finish dancing and he beating pan in the steel band and every now and then jumping up when the weed hit the sky and screaming out for everybody to dance or come and beat pan in the band. Bart drunk as hell and he sitting in a corner holding his head and staring into space. Tanty pulling Tolroy away from his woman saying that she tired and want to go home. Lewis like if he is the happiest man in the hall how he get this divorce from Agnes, and he going to everybody and telling them how he used to thump she every night.

It look as if Moses know everybody in the hall, for it ain't have a fellar who pass what didn't ask him what happening.

'How you know so much people, boy?' Galahad ask.

'I didn't come to London yesterday,' Moses say. 'I was among the first set of spades what come to Brit'n. And then, it ain't have so many places the boys could go to, so you bound to meet them up sooner or later. Long time was the old Paramount in Tottenham Court Road. I mean, them was days. It don't have nothing like that again.'

'Better fete than this?' Galahad ask.

'Better fete than this!' Moses say. 'Boy, this ain't nothing. The boys used to overflow into the road when it had a lime there on a Saturday. One time a Jamaican fellar take off all his clothes to fight an Irishman opposite a pub there. And talk about weed! Everybody used to be as high as the sky.'

'You ever hit a weed Moses?'

'Sure I hit a weed, I do everything for experience.'

'How you feel when you smoke it?'

'At first you feel bad but afterwards like nothing matter in the world. You will die laughing at anything, and you feel as if you walking on air. But I don't bother with that again. One year I was working in the Post Office—every year around Christmas time they does take on fellars to help with the work—and it had a Jamaican who used to hit the weed regularly at work. I used to pass by him and say, "Ah papa, like you high!" and he used to look at me and smile.'

'You know where to get? I would like to try one.'

'It have plenty of trouble in that, but the way how you ask me remind me about them English fellars. Is a funny thing, but sometimes you walking down the road and all them who you pass ask you the same thing. They like the weed more than anybody else, and from the time they see you black they figure that you know all about it, where to make contact and how much to pay. But I not in that racket. In fact I don't know any of the boys who in it, though now and then you would see them high. If you want to have a go you better ask Five when he come down to earth.'

Big City and Five come up to them during a break and all of them went to the bar to have a drink.

'This man Harris only fast!' Five say. 'Distinguish guest! How you don't know I fix up a little thing with the skin? Who you think taking she home when the fete over?'

'But what about all them girls you bring with you?' Galahad ask.

Five wave his hand in the air. 'One today, one tomorrow,' he say. 'Listen, any of them you like you could have. Daniel!' he call out to the other end of the bar, 'you treating the girls right?' Daniel stick his thumb up in the air like them RAF fellars and smile. 'That man is a real friend,' Five say. 'How you make out with the other one, City?'

'As you say,' Big City answer, 'Harris only fast. But she don't want to leave the other girl, so we will have to go together.'

'That is all right, boy,' Five say, 'anything goes. Jesus Christ, it making hot in here, though. What happen Moses, I ain't see you dancing?'

'I had one or two,' Moses say, 'But you know the old man, always taking things easy.'

'How your head, Five?' Galahad ask.

'It all right, man, it only break a cocacola bottle. You know, I would have beaten that — if youall didn't hold me back. But we make back friends after.'

Harris come to the bar as if nothing happen and order a lemonade.

'What time this fete overing, Harris?' Five ask him.

'At the usual time, half-past eleven,' Harris say.

'Oh Christ,' Five say, 'I don't know why in a big city like London you can't have a fete till morning. Look how it is back home, they have non-stop dance, you dance till you fall down on the ground, the moon go, the sun come, evening come, night come again and still the boys on the floor. Why the arse

London Transport can't run bus and tube all night for people to go home?'

'I wish you would watch your language,' Harris say. 'You don't know it, but there are decent people around you.'

'Yes,' Big City say, 'stop —ing up a good time, Five.'

'Take it easy boys,' Moses say.

'Another thing,' Harris say, drinking the lemonade and forgetting to speak proper English for a minute, 'is when the fete finish and the band playing God Save The Queen, some of you have a habit of walking about as if the fete still going on, and you, Five, the last time you come to one of my dances you was even jocking waist when everybody else was standing at attention. Now it have decent people here tonight, and if you don't get on respectable it will be a bad reflection not only on me but on all the boys, and you know how things hard already in Brit'n. The English people will say we are still uncivilised and don't know how to behave properly. So please boys, do me a favour, and when the band play God Save The Queen, stand up to attention.'

'All right Mr Harris,' Five say, 'anything you want. If you want me to leave right now I will leave.' Then he change his tone. 'Come and have a drink with the boys, man. You haven't had one for the night.'

'You know I don't drink,' Harris say.

'Ah, that is now, but you remember them days in Port of Spain when—'

But Harris went away before Five could finish stirring up the memories, to tell the other boys to remember to stand still when the band playing God Save The Queen.

*　　*　　*

It had one bitter season, when it look like the vengeance of Moko fall on all the boys in London, nobody can't get any work, fellars who had work losing it, and all over the place it look like if Operation Pressure gone into execution in a big way.

Galahad for one lose his work, and though it was winter—a real grim one with pipe bursting and people carrying bucket to the road standpipe like in the West Indies to draw water—the old Galahad not very much affected by the weather. Some miracle of metabolism was still keeping him warm at a time when normal people rattling with cold, and while they bawling and shivering he was able to walk about the streets in an ordinary suit of clothing, sympathising with the huddlers and shiverers in the blast of wind that does sometimes sweep across the city like a vengeance angel. Fellars put him down for mad, seeing him dress like that in the winter, and as for the Nordics, some of them stare at this spade who defying the elements as if he is a witch doctor.

Galahad used to go walking in Kensington Gardens, the fog never clear enough for him to see down to High Street Ken. That particular winter, things was so bad with him that he had was to try and catch a pigeon in the park to eat. It does have a lot of them flying about, and the people does feed them with bits of bread. Sometimes they get so much bread that they pick and choosing, and Galahad watching them with envy. In this country, people prefer to see man starve than a cat or dog want something to eat.

Watching these fat pigeons strut about the park, the idea come to Galahad to snatch one and take it home and roast it. When he was a little fellar his father had a work in High Street in San Fernando, a town about forty miles from Port of Spain. It used to have pigeons like stupidness all about the street—nobody know where they come from, and Galahad father used to snatch and send them home to cook.

Galahad remember that as he stand up there by the pond in the gardens, watching the people throw bread for the swans, and hold pieces for the seagulls to swoop down and take it. Which part these seagulls come from? he wonder, for he always think that seagulls belong to the sea.

Once the idea come to his head, he begin to go to the park

regularly to study pigeon life, to watch the movements and plan out a strategy. It have a little place, near an entrance to the park (as soon as you cross over the zebra, a little way down from Queensway) where the pigeons does hang out a lot. Only thing is that it have iron railing there, so you can't get right up to the birds. But people like to stand there and throw bread for them, and they does come near to the railing, so if you really desperate you could push your hand in and snatch one.

Was that what Galahad plan to do, and he wasn't so much frighten of the idea of the snatch as what would happen if one of them animal-loving people see him. That thought make him shiver, and the morning he was in action he look around carefully to make sure nobody near.

'Coo-coo,' Galahad say, throwing bread and leaning on the rail.

'Coo-coo-coo,' the pigeons say, and they start to flutter around as Galahad throw bread, for it was early in the morning and the usual bread-givers wasn't out yet.

Galahad eye a fat fellar who edging up to the rail. He start to drop bread a little nearer, until the bird was close. He make the snatch so quietly that the other pigeons only flutter around a little and went on eating. He start to swing the pigeon around, holding it by the head, for he want to kill it quick and push it in his pocket.

As aforesaid, that particular season it was as if the gods against the boys, and just as Galahad swinging the pigeon one of them old geezers who does always wear furcoat come through the entrance with little Flossie on a lead, to give the little dear a morning constitution, and as soon as Flossie spot the spade she start a sharp barking.

'Oh you cruel, cruel beast!' the woman say, and Galahad head fly back from where he kneeling on the ground to handle the situation better. 'You cruel monster! You killer!'

Galahad blood run cold: he see the gallows before him right away and he push the pigeon in his jacket pocket and stand up, and the pigeon still fluttering in the pocket.

'I must find a policeman!' the woman screech, throwing her hands up in the air, and she turn back to the road.

Galahad make races through the park, heading down for Lancaster Gate.

Later in the morning, he went round by Moses.

'I buy a bird, boy,' he tell Moses. 'Get up and let we make a cook.'

'You buy a bird!' Moses say. 'Where you get money from to buy bird, papa?' But the idea of eating a bird and rice have him out of bed long time.

Now when Galahad did reach back home, and he sit down and start to pick the bird feather, he start to feel guilty. All he try to argue with himself that he only do it because he hungry and things brown, still the feeling that he do a bad thing wouldn't leave him. 'What the hell I care,' he say to himself, 'so much damn pigeon all about the place. Look how they making mess all about in Trafalgar Square until the government trying to get rid of them. What the hell happen if I snatch one to eat?' But when he finish plucking the pigeon conscious humbugging him so much that he fling it in a corner. Little later he thought about Moses. 'Moses in this country long,' he say to himself, 'and if he could eat it I don't see why I must feel so guilty.' So he went round by Moses.

'I make a snatch,' Galahad say, and he tell Moses all what happen.

'Boy, you take a big chance,' Moses say. 'You think this is Trinidad? Them pigeons there to beautify the park, not to eat. The people over here will kill you if you touch a fly.' But all the same the old Moses eyeing the bird, and is a nice, fat one. 'Well, clean it and cut it up,' he say, 'I will put the rice on to boil. But you mustn't do this kind of thing again, you will get in big trouble.'

'The old geezer call me a cruel monster,' Galahad say. 'If you did see she face, you would think I commit a murder.'

'You lucky they didn't catch you,' Moses say.

'Is a long time I ain't eat pigeon, boy,' Galahad say.

'Pigeon meat really sweet,' Moses say.

In about a hour they was eating pigeon and rice. Galahad sucking the bones and smacking his lips.

'You have a cigarette?' he ask Moses when he finish.

'Look some Benson there on the table—Cap was round here yesterday.'

'How things going at the factory?' Galahad say, lighting up and sitting back. Then he say, 'You have the room too hot, man. Turn down the gas a little.'

'You all right, yes,' Moses say, 'something wrong with you.'

'Boy, work hard like hell to get these days. Day before yesterday I scout the Great West Road, by all them factory, and nothing doing nowhere at all. It look like they clamping down on the boys hard.'

'I hear a Indian fellar say it have work in a cigarette factory in the East End, but I don't know. They might take Indian and not spades. You could go and try if you like. Is just a little way from Aldgate.'

'How much they paying?'

'You could hit a tens with overtime.'

'I might go and try. Is when you think Lyons will begin taking fellars down in Cadby Hall?'

'Well last year we had a good spring and they start about March. But it all depend on the weather, people don't want ice cream when it so cold.'

'Boy, when you not working you does feel bad.'

Moses light a cigarette and sit down before the fire.

'That —ing skylight still leaking,' he say, looking up as he lean back in the chair. 'I try to put some putty yesterday, but the water still coming through.'

'Why you don't tell the landlord about it?'

'I tell him already, man, but you know how these fellars is. I take the broom and put a rag on it and wipe the glass, and that help a little. Sometimes the heat from the fire make water on the glass.'

'You hear from home lately?'

'No man. I write my brother and tell him to send £500 for me, but I ain't get a reply. You hear?'

'I get a letter from a fellar yesterday who say he want to come up.'

'All them fellars want to come up. They must be think life easy here.'

'They don't know.'

The pigeon and rice have Moses feeling good and he in the mood for a oldtalk.

'Aye Galahad,' he say, 'you used to know a fellar name Brackley in Charlotte Street?'

'Brackley? Charlotte Street? But how you mean? You think I would be living in Port of Spain and don't know Brackley! Ain't he is the fellar who ain't have no nose, and he always riding about town on a ladies bicycle, peddling with his heels, and his fingers sticking out on the handle bars? And if you tell him anything he curse you like hell?'

'Yes! Just as I was sitting down here I remember Brackley. Boy, he was one test could make you laugh! If you call out to him he stop the bike and start to curse you. "What the — you want? What the — you calling me for? Brackley is your father?"'

Galahad laugh. 'Yes, I know. You ever hear bout the time when Brackley sleep with a whore?'

'No.'

'It was Tina. It was a Tuesday night, so things was really bad with the girls, and Brackley broach Tina. She say all right, but only thing Brackley must get up early in the morning and out off, because she don't want them other girls to know she sleep with a fellar like him. Brackley agree, and Tina carry him home in George Street and they went to sleep. Next morning Tina get up very early and gone in the market for her fresh piece of beef, thinking that by the time she come back Brackley

would be gone. But Brackley take time and get up, and start to
yawn and stretch, and he open the window and stand up there
scratching his chest. All them whores in the backyard looking
at Brackley and saying: "A-a! Brackley sleep with Tina, me
child!" And Brackley stand up there waving his hand: "Morning neighbour! morning!" and laughing all over his face. When
Tina come back she start to kick up hell, but Brackley say,
"What the hell happen to you? I give you my money and I
sleep with you and everybody know." '

Moses laugh. 'You hear bout the time they nail Brackley to
the cross?' he ask Galahad.

'No.'

'One Sunday morning they nail Brackley to the cross up on
Calvary Hill. You know where that is? Up there behind the
Dry River, as you going up Laventille. Well it had a gang of
wayside preachers, and Brackley join them, and he decide this
morning to make things look real. So he tell them to nail him
to the cross before they start to preach. Brackley stretch out
there, and they drive nails between his fingers and tie up his
hands with twine. Brackley look as if he really suffering. A
test went and get a bucket of cattle blood and throw it over him,
and Brackley hang up there while the wayside preachers start
to preach. The leader take out a white sheet and spread it on
the ground, and three-four women stand up with hymnbook in
their hand, and they singing and preaching. But them boys
start to make rab. They begin with little pebbles, but they gradually increase to some big brick. Brick flying all by Brackley head
until he start to bawl, "Take me down from here!" Brackley
shout. "They didn't stone Christ on the cross!" And this time
big macadam and rock flying all about in the air.'

Galahad laugh until tears come, and Moses suddenly sober
up, as if it not right that in these hard times he and Galahad
could sit there, belly full with pigeon, smoking cigarette, and
talking bout them characters back home. As if Moses get a
guilty feeling, and he watch Galahad with sorrow, thinking

that he ain't have no work and the winter upon the city.

'Boy,' Moses say, 'look how we sit down here happy, and things brown in general. I mean, sometimes when we oldtalking so I does wonder about the boys, how all of we come up to the old Brit'n to make a living, and how years go by and we still here in this country. Things like that does bother me. With this night work, sometimes I get up all around eleven o'clock in the morning—'

'So you wouldn't miss elevenses,' Galahad say.

'I talking serious, man. And I can't go back to sleep, I just lay there on the bed thinking about my life, how after all these years I ain't get no place at all, I still the same way, neither forward nor backward. You take my advice, Galahad. Is how long you in the country now?'

'Three-four years.'

'Ah, yes.' Moses lean back in the old armchair the Polish landlord give him—that is to say, Moses see the armchair in the landing and put it in his room—and a look come in his face that bring all the years of suffering to light. 'When was my second winter here, I was still ready to go back home. I used to go by them shipping offices and find out what ships leaving for Trinidad, just in case I happen to raise the money. How long you think I in Brit'n now, Galahad?'

'Five years?'

'Ten years, papa, ten years the old man in Brit'n, and what to show for it? What happen during all that time? From winter to winter, summer to summer, work after work. Sleep, eat, hustle pussy, work. Boy, sometimes I sit there and think about that, think about it real hard. Look how it is, them Jamaican fellars who only here for two-three years save up enough money to send for their family and I ain't have cent in the bank. How them fellars manage to save money on five-six pounds a week beat me, and yet they do it. Boy, if I was you, I would save up my money and when you have a little thing put by, hustle back to Trinidad.'

'Who me? No boy. I not going back.'

'Ah, you just like Daniel and Five Past Twelve and them other fellars. You know what they say? They say that if they have money they would go all about on the continent, and live big, and they would never leave Brit'n. Boy, you know what I want to do? I want to go back to Trinidad and lay down in the sun and dig my toes, and eat a fish broth and go Maracas Bay and talk to them fishermen, and all day long I sleeping under a tree, with just the old sun for company. You know what I would do if I had money? I go and live Paradise—you know where Paradise is? Is somewhere between St Joseph and Tacarigua, is a small village, one time it had a Portugee fellar name Jesus there and he had a rumshop, so Ripley had him in Believe It Or Not —Jesus have a rumshop in Paradise. Anyway up there life real easy. I would get a old house and have some cattle and goat, and all day long sit down in the grass in the sun, and hit a good corn cuckoo and calaloo now and then. That is life for me, boy. I don't want no ballet and opera and symphony.'

'You know,' Galahad say, 'last year I had a feeling to go back too, but I forget about it. It ain't have no prospects back home, boy.'

'Sometimes I look back on all the years I spend in Brit'n,' Moses say, 'and I surprise that so many years gone by. Looking at things in general life really hard for the boys in London. This is a lonely miserable city, if it was that we didn't get together now and then to talk about things back home, we would suffer like hell. Here is not like home where you have friends all about. In the beginning you would think that is a good thing, that nobody minding your business, but after a while you want to get in company, you want to go to somebody house and eat a meal, you want to go on excursion to the sea, you want to go and play football and cricket. Nobody in London does really accept you. They tolerate you, yes, but you can't go in their house and eat or sit down and talk. It ain't have no sort of family life for us here. Look at Joseph. He married to a

English girl and they have four children, and they living in two rooms in Paddington. He apply to the LCC for a flat, but it look like he would never get one. Now the children big enough to go to school, and what you think? Is big fight every day because the other children calling them darkie. When they not at school they in the street playing. Boy, when I was a little fellar my mother cut my tail if I play in the street. And you think Joseph could make out on that six pounds ten he getting? As it is he have ten pounds for me and I feel bad to ask him for it when I meet him. Boy, when I see thing like that happening to other people I decide I would never married. Look what happen to Lewis, how his wife divorce him.'

'Lewis look for that, thumping the woman every night.'

'Yes, but still. And another thing, look how people does dead and nobody don't know nothing until the milk bottles start to pile up in front of the door. Supposing one day I keel off here in this room? I don't take milk regular—I would stay here until one of the boys drop round. That is a hell of a thing to think about, you know. One time a test dead in this house— right there down the hall, in the second room. You know what? I miss the test—was one of them old geezers, every morning she see me she say. "Cold today, isn't it? I bet you wish you were back home now." She used to wear a fur coat and go in the park and sit down, crouch up like a fowl when rain falling. Well I miss the test: when I ask the landlord for her, he say she dead about a month ago. You see what I mean?'

'The best thing to do is to take milk regular,' Galahad say.

'Laugh kiff-kiff if you want, but I here in this country longer than you, and you still have a lot to learn. You never leave the gas fire on by mistake?'

'No. I only use it when I cooking.'

'Oh, I forget you don't want heat in the winter. Anyway you don't read the papers? Every day somebody dead with leaving gas on. If a test don't like your head, all he have to do is come in the room when you sleeping and put on the gas, and next day you get two lines in the newspaper.'

'The trouble with you,' Galahad say, 'is that you want a holiday. Why you don't take a trip to Berlin or Moscow? Listen, I hear the Party giving free trips to the boys to go to different cities on the continent, with no strings attached, you don't have to join up or anything.'

'Who tell you so?'

'I get a wire. I hear two students went, and they say they had a sharp time, over there not like London at all, the people greeting you with open arms. Why you don't contact the Party?'

'Take it easy, I have enough grey hairs as it is. But talking about holiday, what does happen here when is Christmas? No fete at all, everybody in the house eating Christmas pudding. Boy, you remember what Christmas does be like back home? Fete like stupidness. And right after that come New Year. They don't celebrate that in this country at all, though I always want to take a trip to bonny Scotland, I hear Old Years is big fete there.'

'Who tell you they don't celebrate here?'

'Ah, bags of people stand up in the Circus and throw balloon in the air—you call that fete? The only thing is them white girls does want to kiss you. They say if the first thing they do for the new year is see a spade, they will have luck for the whole year. Them bastards!'

'It good to lime out there every Old Year,' Galahad say.

'To do what? Get a kiss? Man, you really foolish, yes. Fellars like you would stay in Brit'n till you dead. You come like a old spade I know. He living down Ladbroke Grove. He come to this country since he was a young man, full of ambition, and he never went back. He had some good times, yes, but what you think happen to him in old age? If you see him now, crouching about in them tube station in a old beast coat, and picking cigarette butt from the pavement. Study for old age, boy. Study what will happen to you if you stay here and get old. Boy, if I was sure that I would get a good job in Trinidad, and

I had my passage back home, you think I will stay here? But is no use talking to fellars like you. You hit two-three white women and like you gone mad.'

'I don't know why you shouting down the old country like that,' Galahad say. 'If you ain't do well is nobody fault but your own. Look at all them other fellars who do all right for themselves. Look at the students—'

'Don't talk about students,' Moses say. 'That is another thing altogether. Them fellars have their bread buttered from home, they ain't come to Brit'n to hustle like you and me. They spend a few years here, learn a profession, then go back home stupider than when they come. They go back with English wife and what happen? As soon as they get there, the places where their white wife could go, they can't go. Next thing you hear, the wife horning them and the marriage gone puff. Look what happen to that Indian fellar what married a German girl and went back after he study. He kill the girl, cut she up and put she in a sack and throw she in the sea. You don't know about that case?'

'I hear about it.'

'That was a big thing, man. They even send detective to London to check up fingerprint and thing. You should know in the end they hang the test, and the boys make a big calypso out of it.'

'What I mean,' Galahad say, 'is the impression on the English people how the papers always talking about fellars coming up here to work and creating problem. I mean, it have a lot of other fellars who come to study and visit and so on. It ain't only hustlers like we.'

'Yes, but nobody interested in them fellars.'

'We had better chances when the Socialists was in power, you know. You ever vote?'

'But how you mean? I always go and put my X, man. And I always canvassing for Labour when is elections.'

'Boy, you think fellars like Daniel and Harris does vote Conservative or Labour?'

'I suspect Harris, you know. He tell me Labour, but I have a mind he is a Tory at heart. He always talking about the greatness of the old Churchill and how if it wasn't for him this country go right down.'

'Well,' Galahad get up, 'we will pick up. I have to go to school this afternoon to collect the rent.'

'If you happen to see Cap,' Moses say, getting ready to go back to sleep, 'tell him to pass around by me.'

*   *   *

It have a p.s. episode with the pigeons what happen to Cap, and he never tell any of the boys because he fraid they laugh at him. What happen was this: One time in his migrations Cap was staying in a top room in Dawson Place, near the Gate, and for some reason or other seagulls start to sleep in the night on a ledge up by the roof. These seagulls that come up from the old Thames when things too hard for them by the sea, you could never tell where you will see them. Sometimes they join the pigeons in Trafalgar Square, and it have some of them does hang out by the Odeon in Marble Arch. Anyway, nobody surprise to see seagulls sitting up there on the roof, and in fact how Cap get to find out is because one day he had a girl in the room, and he went out and forget to take the key. So when he come back he ring the bell, and as is the habit with the fellars who living in top room, whoever there would open the window and throw the key down for the person outside instead of climbing down all them stairs to open the door. So when Cap ring the bell, the girl open the window to throw the key, and when Cap look up he see these seagulls flying about and settling on the roof.

However, he didn't think about it again until much later, when he was laying down on the bed after the girl left. In fact, he fall asleep and get up in the evening feeling so hungry that his head giddy and he frighten to get out of bed and exert himself. Cap lay there thinking about big meals at Chinese and Indian restaurants, and remembering the times when fortune favour him and his belly full so he didn't have to worry about food. And while he was in this meditation, the seagulls start to fly across his mind.

Cap leap out of bed and fly by the window. Sure enough, the ledge passing near the window and a good stretch could bring him in contact with the gulls. Cap get so excited that he make a wild snatch and catch a seagull by the tail. The seagull cry out and flutter out of his grasp, leaving him with two feathers in his hand.

Now them seagull not as tame as the pigeons in London, and from the time Cap make the wild attack they all move out of range. Cap went back and lay down on the bed, for he does think best in that position.

Then he leap up again and went in the cupboard to look for bread. He find an end slice and he break it up in little bits. All this action getting him hungrier and hungrier and he contemplating how seagull would taste, for he never eat one before.

When the bread break up Cap find a piece of long twine in a drawer and he make a slippery knot. He went and open the window again and put the twine down, making a circle, and in the circle he put a few pieces of bread and he jam himself up against the wall, just twisting his head so he could see what happening.

Two-three seagulls come, but instead of settling they hover in the air like hummingbird and eat all the bread. Cap put more bread and wait. This time two come and one of them that was greedy decide to settle down and eat off all the bread.

As soon as the bird foot touch the ledge Cap make the pull. The seagull jump up a little, as if it playing skip with Cap, and when the twine fly underneath—Cap pull real hard—it settle down again.

Cap throw away the twine in a corner and went and lay down again, the old brain wrestling with the problem. Then he leap up again and take up a old cardboard box. He went and take his clothes off the hanger. He tie the twine to the hanger. He open the window, and he prop up the box with the hanger, and he put bread in the space under the box and jam up against the wall to wait, holding the other end of the twine in his fingers.

Two seagull come to investigate and they see the bread and start to eat. As soon as one was under the box, Cap jerk the string, the hanger fall and the cardboard box fall on a seagull.

The old Cap, frighten that the bird might get away, drag the box in through the window, keeping it down.

When Cap pull the box in it fall down inside and the seagull start to fly about in Cap room. He shut the window quick and stand up there watching the bird. He know for sure that he have it now, so he just stand up there enjoying anticipation, waiting for a good chance to catch it.

The seagull went on Cap bed and stand up there on the pillow, watching him, the head nodding and the eyes bright.

'Quee-quee,' Cap say, taking a piece of bread in his hand and holding it out like the people in the park.

'Quee-quee-quee,' the seagull say, but it make no move to go to Cap.

Cap drop the bread and make a dive for the bed. He nearly catch it that time, and he thought he had, but when he look is a feather from the tail that he holding.

Now the bird start to fly round and round the room, making circle with the electric light in the centre.

But hunger have Cap desperate now and he making some wild grab that almost catching the bird, but the bird making some kind of fancy swerve every time and getting away.

Cap get so vex that he take a blanket off the bed, and he wait until the seagull coming around in the circle, and he throw the blanket. He bring the bird down, tangle up in the blanket, and he throw himself on the blanket and hold down the bird.

In the two weeks that Cap stay in that top room, he lessen the seagull population in London evening after evening. Not to arouse suspicion he used to put the feathers in a paper bag and when he go out in the night, throw it in a garden or a public rubbish bin.

The menu had him looking well, he eat seagull in all manner and fashion. He recover his strength, and when the landlord tell him that he had to leave, Cap cast a sorrowful glance upwards when he was leaving Dawson Place.

The next place that he went to live, he get a top room again when he ask for it, but seagulls never come on that ledge, though Cap used to put bread out every day.

*　　*　　*

The changing of the seasons, the cold slicing winds, the falling leaves, sunlight on green grass, snow on the land, London particular. Oh what it is and where it is and why it is, no one knows, but to have said: 'I walked on Waterloo Bridge,' 'I rendezvoused at Charing Cross,' 'Piccadilly Circus is my playground,' to say these things, to have lived these things, to have lived in the great city of London, centre of the world. To one day lean against the wind walking up the Bayswater Road (destination unknown), to see the leaves swirl and dance and spin on the pavement (sight unseeing), to write a casual letter home beginning: 'Last night, in Trafalgar Square...'

What it is that a city have, that any place in the world have, that you get so much to like it you wouldn't leave it for anywhere else? What it is that would keep men although by and large, in truth and in fact, they catching their royal to make a living, staying in a cramp-up room where you have to do everything—sleep, eat, dress, wash, cook, live. Why it is, that although they grumble about it all the time, curse the people, curse the government, say all kind of thing about this and that, why it is, that in the end, everyone cagey about saying outright that if the chance come they will go back to them green islands in the sun?

In the grimness of the winter, with your hand plying space like a blind man's stick in the yellow fog, with ice on the ground and a coldness defying all effort to keep warm, the boys coming and going, working, eating, sleeping, going about the vast metropolis like veteran Londoners.

Nearly every Sunday morning, like if they going to church, the boys liming in Moses room, coming together for a oldtalk, to find out the latest gen, what happening, when is the next fete, Bart asking if anybody see his girl anywhere, Cap recounting a episode he had with a woman by the tube station the night before, Big City want to know why the arse he can't win a pool, Galahad recounting a clash with the colour problem in a restaurant in Piccadilly, Harris saying he hope the weather turns, Five saying he have to drive a truck to Glasgow tomorrow.

Always every Sunday morning they coming to Moses, like if is confession, sitting down on the bed, on the floor, on the chairs, everybody asking what happening but nobody like they know what happening, laughing kiff-kiff at a joke, waiting to see who would start to smoke first, asking Moses if he have any thing to eat, the gas going low, why you don't put another shilling in, who have shilling, anybody have change? And everybody turning out their pockets for this shilling that would mean the difference between shivering and feeling warm, and nobody having any shilling, until conscious hit one of them and he say: 'Aps! Look I have a shilling, it was right down in the bottom of my trousers pocket, and I didn't feel it.'

'Boy Moses, if I tell you what happen to me last night—'

'Boy, you hear of any work anywhere?'

'Man, I looking for a room.'

'Boy, I pick up something by the Arch yesterday—'

Sometimes during the week, when he come home and he can't sleep, is as if he hearing the voices in the room, all the moaning and groaning and sighing and crying, and he open his eyes expecting to see the boys sitting around.

Sometimes, listening to them, he look in each face, and he feel a great compassion for every one of them, as if he live each of their lives, one by one, and all the strain and stress come to rest on his own shoulders.

'What you doing, Moses? You still thinking about going back home?'

'I see they have a lot of tinned breadfruit about the place.'

'—and if was me I would of thump she—'

'Moses, how you so quiet, like time catching up with you, boy.'

'So what happening these days?'

Some Sunday mornings he hardly say a word, he only lay there on the bed listening to them talk about what happen last night, and Harris looking at his watch anxiously and saying that he has an important engagement, but all the same never getting up to go, and Bart saying that he sure one of the boys must have seen his girl Beatrice, but you-all too nasty, you wouldn't tell me where, ease me up, man, I must find that girl again, and Cap smiling his innocent smile what trap so many people, and Galahad cocky and pushing his mouth in everything and Big City fiddling with the radio (Radio Luxembourg always have good fusic), and if Five in town he want to know who going to lime in the evening.

'Moses, if you hear of anything, let me know, eh.'

'Boy, it have any rooms down here? Two fellars coming up next week and I can't get a place for them—you could help me out?'

'I hear that they looking for the boys to do National Service —watch out, Galahad, you still twenty.'

Sometimes, after they gone, he hear the voices ringing in his ear, and sometimes tears come to his eyes and he don't know why really, if is home-sickness or if is just that life in general beginning to get too hard.

How many Sunday mornings gone like that? It look to him
as if life composed of Sunday morning get-togethers in the room:
he must make a joke of it during the week and say: 'You
coming to church Sunday?' Lock up in that small room, with
London and life on the outside, he used to lay there on the bed,
thinking how to stop all of this crap, how to put a spoke in the
wheel, to make things different. Like how he tell Cap to get to
hell out one night, so he should do one Sunday morning when
he can't bear it any more: Get to hell out, why the arse you
telling me about how they call you a darkie, you think I am
interested?

Dress, go out, coast a lime in the park. Walking that way, he
might meet up Harris and Galahad, both of them dress like
Englishmen, with bowler hat and umbrella, and the *Times*
sticking out of the jacket pocket so the name would show.

Hello boy, what happening.

So what happening, man, what happening.

How long you in Brit'n boy?

You think this winter bad? You should of been here in '52.

What happening, what happening man.

What the arse happening, lord? What all of us doing, coasting
lime, Galahad asking if anybody know the words of the song
Maybe It's Because I'm A Londoner, Cap want two pounds
borrow, Five only in town for the night and he want to know
if he could sleep in Moses room, Big City coming tomorrow to
full up the coupons (I nearly hit them last week), Lewis saying
that Agnes come begging and if he should go to live with her
again, Tolroy want to send Ma and Tanty back to Jamaica
(them two old bitches, I don't know why they don't dead).

So what happening, Tolroy? I don't see you with your guitar
these days?

Every year he vowing to go back to Trinidad, but after the
winter gone and birds sing and all the trees begin to put on
leaves again, and flowers come and now and then the old sun
shining, is as if life start all over again, as if it still have time,

as if it still have another chance. I will wait until after the summer, the summer does really be hearts.

But it reach a stage, and he know it reach that stage, where he get so accustom to the pattern that he can't do anything about it. Sure, I could do something about it, he tell himself, but he never do anything. He used to wonder about back home, where he have a grandmother and a girl friend who always writing him and asking him why he don't come back, that they would go and live in Grenada, where her father have a big estate.

Why you don't go back to Trinidad.

What happening man, what happening.

If I give you this ballad! Last night—

You went to see the Christmas tree in Trafalgar Square?

Harris giving a dance in Brixton next Saturday—you going?

A fellar asking the Home Secretary in the House of Commons: 'Are you aware that there are more than 40,000 West Indians living in Great Britain?'

'You know who I see in Piccadilly last night? Gomes! He must be come up for talks of federation.'

One night of any night, liming on the Embankment near to Chelsea, he stand up on the bank of the river, watching the lights of the buildings reflected in the water, thinking what he must do, if he should save up money and go back home, if he should try to make it by next year before he change his mind again.

The old Moses, standing on the banks of the Thames. Sometimes he think he see some sort of profound realisation in his life, as if all that happen to him was experience that make him a better man, as if now he could draw apart from any hustling and just sit down and watch other people fight to live. Under the kiff-kiff laughter, behind the ballad and the episode, the what-happening, the summer-is-hearts, he could see a great aimlessness, a great restless, swaying movement that leaving you standing in the same spot. As if a forlorn shadow of doom fall on all the spades in the country. As if he could see the black faces bobbing up and down in the millions of white, strained faces, everybody hustling along the Strand, the spades jostling in the crowd, bewildered, hopeless. As if, on the surface, things don't look so bad, but when you go down a little, you bounce up a kind of misery and pathos and a frightening—what? He don't know the right word, but he have the right feeling in his heart. As if the boys laughing, but they only laughing because they fraid to cry, they only laughing because to think so much about everything would be a big calamity—like how he here now, the thoughts so heavy like he unable to move his body.

Still, it had a greatness and a vastness in the way he was feeling tonight, like it was something solid after feeling everything else give way, and though he ain't getting no happiness out of the cogitations he still pondering, for is the first time that he ever find himself thinking like that.

Daniel was telling him how over in France all kinds of fellars writing books what turning out to be best-sellers. Taxi-driver, porter, road-sweeper—it didn't matter. One day you sweating in the factory and the next day all the newspapers have your name and photo, saying how you are a new literary giant.

He watch a tugboat on the Thames, wondering if he could ever write a book like that, what everybody would buy.

It was a summer night: laughter fell softly: it was the sort of night that if you wasn't making love to a woman you feel you was the only person in the world like that.

Other Titles Available

Longman African Writers

A Forest of Flowers	K Saro-Wiwa	0 582 27320 X
Tides	I Okpewho	0 582 10276 6
Of Men and Ghosts	K Aidoo	0 582 22871 9
Flowers and Shadows	B Okri	0 582 03536 8
Violence	F Iyayi	0 582 00240 0
The Victims	I Okpewho	0 582 00241 9
Call Me Not a Man	M Matshoba	0 582 00242 7
The Beggar's Strike	A Sowfall	0 582 00243 5
Dilemma Of a Ghost / Anowa	A A Aidoo	0 582 00244 3
Our Sister Killjoy	A A Aidoo	0 582 00391 1
No Sweetness Here	A A Aidoo	0 582 00393 8
The Marriage of Anansewa / Edufa	E Sutherland	0 582 00245 1
The Cockroach Dance	M Mwangi	0 582 00392 X
Muriel At Metropolitan	M Tlali	0 582 01657 6
The Children of Soweto	M Mzamane	0 582 01680 0
A Son Of The Soil	W Katiyo	0 582 02656 3
The Stillborn	Z Alkali	0 582 02657 1
The Life of Olaudah Equiano	P Edwards	0 582 03070 6
Sundiata	D T Niane	0 582 64259 0
The Last Duty	I Okpewho	0 582 78535 9
Tales of Amadou Koumba	B Diop	0 582 78587 1
Native Life South Africa	S Plaatje	0 582 78589 8
Hungry Flames	M Mzamane	0 582 78590 1
Scarlet Song	M Ba	0 582 78595 2
Fools	N Ndebele	0 582 78621 5
Master and Servant	D Mulwa	0 582 78632 0
The Park	J Matthews	0 582 04080 9
Man Pass Man	N Mokoso	0 582 01681 9
Hurricane of Dust	A Djoleto	0 582 01682 7
Heroes	F Iyayi	0 582 78603 7
Loyalties	A Maja-Pearce	0 582 78628 2
Sugarcane With Salt	J Ng'ombe	0 582 05204 1
Study Guide to 'Scarlet Song'	M Ba	0 582 21979 5

Longman Caribbean Writers

Caribbean New Voices	S Brown (Ed)	0 582 23702 8
Consolation	E G Long	0 582 23913 3
Between Two Seasons	I J Boodhoo	0 582 22869 7
Satellite City	A McKenzie	0 582 08688 4
Karl and Other Stories	V Pollard	0 582 22726 7
Homestretch	V Pollard	0 582 22732 1
Discoveries	J Wickham	0 582 21804 7
Chieftain's Carnival	M Anthony	0 582 21805 5
Dream Stories	E Braithwaite	0 582 09340 6
Arrival of the Snakewoman	O Senior	0 582 03170 2
Summer Lightning	O Senior	0 582 78627 4
The Dragon Can't Dance	E Lovelace	0 582 64231 0
Ways of Sunlight	S Selvon	0 582 64261 2
The Lonely Londoners	S Selvon	0 582 64264 7
A Brighter Sun	S Selvon	0 582 64265 5
Foreday Morning	S Selvon	0 582 03982 7
In the Castle of my Skin	G Lamming	0 582 64267 1
My Bones and My Flute	E Mittelholzer	0 582 78552 9
Black Albino	N Roy	0 582 78563 4
The Children of Sisyphus	O Patterson	0 582 78571 5
The Jumbie Bird	I Khan	0 582 78619 3
Study Guide to The Jumbie Bird	S G-Maharaj	0 582 25652 6
Plays for Today	E Hill *et al*	0 582 78620 7
Old Story Time and Smile Orange	T D Rhone	0 582 78633 9
Study Guide to Old Story Time	M Mottid	0 582 23703 3
Baby Mother and the King of Swords	L Goodison	0 582 05492 3
Two Roads to Mount Joyful	E McKenzie	0 582 07125 9
Voiceprint	S Brown *et al*	0 582 78629 0

All these titles are available from your local bookseller, or can be ordered for you. For further information on these titles, and on study guides available contact, your local Longman agent or Longman International Education, Longman Group Limited, Longman House, Burnt Mill, Harlow, Essex, CM20 2JE, England.